Gandhi in Jerusalem

Gandhi in Jerusalem

iUniverse books may be ordered through booksellers or by contacting:

iUniverse
1663 Liberty Drive
Bloomington, IN 47403
www.iuniverse.com
1-800-Authors (1-800-288-4677)

Because of the dynamic nature of the Internet, any web addresses or links contained in this book may have changed since publication and may no longer be valid. The views expressed in this work are solely those of the author and do not necessarily reflect the views of the publisher, and the publisher hereby disclaims any responsibility for them.

Any people depicted in stock imagery provided by Thinkstock are models, and such images are being used for illustrative purposes only.

Certain stock imagery © Thinkstock.

ISBN: 978-1-4620-0872-8 (sc)
ISBN: 978-1-4620-0870-4 (hc)
ISBN: 978-1-4620-0871-1 (e)

Library of Congress Control Number: 2011908502

Printed in the United States of America

iUniverse rev. date: 06/22/2011

Gandhi in Jerusalem

Kanu Bhatt

iUniverse, Inc.
Bloomington

Preface

One of the prime purposes of writing this play is to contribute my little mite to the noble philosophy of peace between different cultures and religions in light dramatic form. There is absolutely no overt or concealed intension to hurt anybody's feeling that contradicts the declared intention. Readers/viewers are welcome to convey their thought or feeling at <u>kbhatt@cogeco.ca</u>>.

Let me appear to be a smart aleck like many playwrights in admitting that I have deviated from the rule of optimum number of characters and minimal information in any script. The said rule may be relevant in entertainment-oriented plays but not where the range of the theme covers topics between Genesis and future of peace on earth starting with Jerusalem. Believing that we are all children of God a group of multi-ethnic females calling themselves the Daughters of Jerusalem declare their resolve to stay in Jerusalem. There is a fine line between a play being serious and stuffy. The character of Narad would hopefully prevent from the play becoming stuffy.

It was not easy to cover such an ambitious theme within an estimated 90 minutes of playtime.

Reverting to the subject of being a smart aleck when asked to name ten greatest playwrights, Bernard Shaw rattled off ten nomenclatures of his own name. He was equally unique in his preface to any of his plays, some of them as brilliant as his plays - Pygmalion being one such example.

I had the temerity of imitating some of Shaw's didactic techniques and tone. For more authentic dramatic effect, some of the dialogues in this play are composed with the help of Nasreen Bahbah, a multi-lingual Palestinian friend—born, brought up and educated in Canada's multicultural environment and thus a suitable help for a multi-ethnic and creative job. After all, none of these characters in the play spoke King's English. They mostly think in Hindi, Yiddish, Urdu, German, and French and dialogue in English all through the play and while responding to the oracle of God and His response to his daughter, Lilith. It was a challenge to balance the dialogues between pedantic and academic.

However, in view of the sober environment of peace to be created between warring cultures with the aid of fantasy I had to reluctantly ignore the rule of optimum characters and the minimal of information delivered. Any default could create irritation in some readers / viewers for the heaviness of the play if they treat it as a source of entertainment. Such people would never read War and Peace by Tolstoy or such works and may opt for cartoon for the thrill and visual wit. They may not realize that these cartoonists are temperamentally serious with a wicked sense of humour and gift of brevity. A cartoon is the ultimate art form of pointed brevity and giggle. I hope my readers/viewers would bear with my humble deviation from the established ground rules of Dramaturgy. Researching on the life and philosophy of this eminent personage was an intimidating task of historic authenticity watered down to popular lingo. Fabricating the role of living characters was relatively easy with one's creativity. The most challenging part was to create the cartoon character of Narad, a legendry figure – a blend of wicked wit and wisdom. Near the closure of the play the most trying moment was a real life situation that emerged wherein a Jerusalem Muslim mother unsuccessfully sought a sizeable amount of cash for a critical surgery for her infant but was denied by International, Israeli and even Palestinian authorities. It was an irony that an anonymous Jewish father paid the desperate mother without divulging that he had lost his own son in a battle with Palestinians. The climax (to me the anticlimax) is reached when after successful surgery the hugging mother murmurs that when *'my son grows up I would raise him to be shahid – a martyr!* The mixed climax of this real life drama could be construed as the product of brainwashing by fanatics or utterly brutalized psyche affected by the brutality of the occupier. In simple terms it is a sordid tragedy. A cynic may term it as stunt by the Zionists! However dramatic, it was a struggle to incorporate this live occurrence in a satirical play. I am endeavoring to liaise with Israeli writer of the documentary *Precious Life* Slomi Aldar from where I obtained the initial data.

It is a tragic medley of love for one's child and conflict of conscience for one's thanklessness.

Let us imagine the international impact of the play on the dream of bi-ethnic co-existence in the shape of United States of Palestine-Israel. A quick glance at the index of the play may arouse one's intrigue.

The prime inspiration for the play was strengthened in my mind while preparing for my doctoral viva voce at the Bible room where Gandhi used to conduct the Bible studies. The walls of this room were studded with inscriptions from all faiths reflecting Gandhi's esteem for them. It oozed the multiple flavours of Faiths with Gandhi as God's Gardener.

It is fondly hoped that this play would morph into a dramatic rainbow of Gandhian philosophy of international amity blended with Einstein's vision of Israel as a beacon of light among other nations; hopefully integrating the Islamic message of peace and self esteem as conveyed by poet Iqbal and seconded by Albert Schweitzer's Christian reverence for life with a shade of effective appeals of Emile Zola while accusing Israel of its kind of apartheid when with equal stoutness Golda Meir's justifies Israel's right to exist! But the subliminal element of the play is the will of the women of Jerusalem to actualize through a book by two youngsters entitled We *the Daughters of Jerusalem–Here to Stay.* The youthful pair of two camps was influenced by the image of anti-war Lysistrata of classical Greece. The climax of the play is the emergence of Lilith, the alleged first wife of Adam to lead the female residents of heaven to visit Jerusalem.

I owe an apology to the Vedic mythology of India for borrowing their legendary character of Narad, the notorious mischief-maker of heaven. Born out of the mind of Brahma— the creator of the Universe in the Hindu belief system, Narad enriches the play with his mean wisdom!

Some of the essential features of any play are a catchy title to grab the attention, brevity of the massive theme, colloquial dialogues, and most importantly, the element of surprise to overwhelm the audience. Based on the positive experience of producing my maiden play, *Trouble in Heaven staged* at Ottawa, I dared the infrequent practice in Dramaturgy of a character directly addressing the audience. One of the best compliments on this technique was when a member of the audience felt being an invisible actor in this three dimensional format termed as the 'fourth wall'.

The very title of the play could intrigue a passerby aware of Gandhi's assassination and his presumed abode in heaven! One may be intrigued with Gandhi in Jerusalem, a prominent seat of Judaism, Christianity, and Islam! An assassin residing in heaven could further compound the puzzle! Journeying through such features, the play ends with a coup d'état by the female residents of heaven.

In a fantasy the 'mighty' playwright could twist mythology or popular lore to create females governing the United States of Jerusalem-Palestine.

Equally gripping in the play are the dialogues between the assassin and Einstein about the purpose of life and death, his debate on the significance of reverence for life with Schweitzer, Golda Myer's fierce resentment of the accusations of Israeli Apartheid and in outwitting Emile Zola and poet Iqbal.

Similarly, the Buddhist concept of Bodhisattva as elaborated in this play allowing residents a vacation from heaven to earth to serve humanity. It minimizes the dread of death while on earth into the slight inconvenience of packing for a holiday! The urge to serve humanity takes precedence over one's self-centered salvation for which the humans strive all their lives, at times at the expense of their responsibility towards other human beings. Bodhisattva is a musical composition of three octaves of drawing the wisdom of the past and blending it with the dreams of future that creates musical dance of the present. It is the communion of the past, future and present. Its applicability in the play attempts to recoup the ultimate spirituality via the reverence for life to serve the humanity as summed up in an Urdu couplet, 'if there is heaven on earth, it is here, it is here, it is here!'

As expected in any drama a recent development in real life has provided an added mandate as summarized below.

Excuse me, I almost forgot that I am eighty-five years old and am in a bit of a rush to publish the following plays that were scripted over the last fifty years during my busy clinical practice and academic pursuit.

Please allow me to leave unless you wish to accompany me to finalize the following plays for publication soon:

PLAY(i) XANTHIPPE & SOCRATES: A play with a dramatically incompatible couple in classical Athens. Though young, educated at home and hailing from a comfortable home when married Xanthippe was slogging away like most housewives while violently quarrelling against her 'chatterbox' husband. Maybe she was the forerunner of the first liberated female of the Western World! Her husband, a decorated hero was poor, illiterate, and without any source of steady income, thus requiring the family to survive on her dowry while he hobnobbed in Agora with young, wealthy disciples and their Egyptian hetaeras imported for their looks and intellectual facility to chitchat. Though younger Plato had one such companion with a romantic name of Europa, he maintained his tender platonic interest in Xanthippe! The volatile marriage chugged along with the unpaid domestic help of a vile servant Danus, who in one of his monologues admits that he represents Athens at its sublime but mostly at its nadir.

Condemned to death for corrupting the youths of Athens, Socrates was surrounded by weeping followers while he swallowed hemlock with a smile though his favorite disciple Plato, was conspicuously absent. Socrates had forbidden Xanthippe from attending his last moments, dryly mumbling that *he wished to die in peace.* The Athenian gossipers wagged their tongues, giddily smirking that *more likely Plato was busy consoling Xanthippe with gentle kisses! (Ha, ha, ha.)*

Belatedly, when repenting Athenians approach Xanthippe to bless the memorial for Socrates, she walks out mumbling, 'I am a mere rib or woman to sweep, cook, weave, and breed and that too sons. Who am I to accept your honor? I can't stomach your courtesy. '

When they persist for her consent, she yells at them, 'You are the killers; Athens is a gang of killers'. Helpless against their pestering she looks at the sky and pleads, 'Oh Hera, Zeus, save me from these Athenian vultures. Feels like throwing up ...I am not used to their honour.' When incessantly pressured, she runs out and Danus quips 'Think she has gone berserk.'

With a piercing shriek the wild-looking Xanthippe reappears to fall on earth while Danus addresses the audience, 'Didn't I tell you she has gone rabid?'

PLAY (ii) INDIRA GANDHI: In this script that is due for publication, Indira refuses to enter the pearly gates, pleading that her bleeding conscience would not allow her to belong in heaven because of her bodyguards' deed thousands of her innocent countrymen were being massacred in the name of her assassination.

PLAY (iii) RAUL WALLENBERG: In an equally powerful voice, the mother of Raul Wallenberg screams at her sympathizers who plead with her to accept her son's probable demise in Soviet prison. With a strong conviction, she declares, "The man who saved two hundred thousand Jewish lives could never die. My son could never, ever die. Never, never, never." In her consistently strong conviction, she collapses, uttering, "Never, never, never," while the curtain drops reluctantly, echoing the same word with conviction—*never, never, never.* The audience had felt that he was on delicate terms with the wife of the Interior Secretary of Hungary!

A few clinically based premises of my plays include:

PLAY (iii) There is no frigid woman on earth, only a clumsy man in her life.

PLAY (iv) Old flames can be rekindled

PLAY (vi) Intimate communication is communion of souls.

Please stop me before I burst with inflated ego.

Acknowledgment

Throughout the three years that I was researching and scripting *Gandhi in Jerusalem* I have received help from so many persons and agencies, for which I owe them my deep appreciation. As a habitually absent-minded person, I cannot risk omitting any one of them and so I promise to thank them individually.

However, I offer my deep appreciation to my mentors for their constant encouragement. Dr. Mohan Juneja (formerly of McMaster University in the Drama section), Bill Ballentyne (formerly of Ryerson University) and Srini Vasan almost a devotee of Shakespeare, Ms. Lana Bordelo of Oakville and Burlington Theatre Groups for sharing their intimate knowledge and offering apt advise.

I offer my quiet tributes to Shaw, Wilde, and Ibsen for serving as my lifelong role models and some of the authors who inspired this play. Above all, my heartfelt thanks of iUniverse and their editorial staff for all the critique and guidance along with my friend Marta Andrade whom rendered all through the process that led to the production of the book and its marketing.

Lastly, I would like to express my intimate appreciation to my wife, Sushila, for tolerating all of my unavoidable neglect and for her inexhaustible patience. My fond regards to my son, Micky, and his spouse, Carole, as well as to my daughter, Mini, and her husband, Mark. Their kids, Alex and Sophia, continue to inspire me with their mirth for life.

Sources of inspiration for the play

Profiles of Gandhi by Norman Cousins
Gandhi's Religious Thoughts by Margaret Chatterjee
Einstein–The Life and Times by Ronald W. Clark
The Religious Thoughts in Islam by Iqbal Muhammad
My Life by Golda Meir
A Guide to Peace and Conciliation by Rabbi Michel Lerner
The House of Sa'ud from Tradition to Terror by Stephen Schwartz
I Accuse by Irving Westein
Prophets Outcast by Adam Shatz
Still Life with Bombers by David Horovitz
The Two Faces of Islam by Stephen Schwartz
God Has Ninety-Nine Names by Judith Miller
Burned Alive – A Victim of the Law of Men by Souad.
Rumi by S Jonathan
Life on an Israeli Kibbutz by Linda Jacobs Altman
The Middle East, the Opposing Viewpoint by William Dudley
The Place of Tolerance in Islam by Khaled Abou El Fadl
The Islamic Roots of Democratic Pluralism
by Abdualaziz Sachedina
We Just Want to Live Here by Amal Rifa'I & Odelia Ainbinder
The Schweitzer Album by Erica Anderson
My Days with Albert Schweitzer by Frederick Franck

LIST OF CHARACTERS

Omnipresent God:: Who apparently spoke back stage.

Except for Gandhi and Narad, all characters wear Greek togas with tiny wings on their angelic shoulders.

Narad: (*Wearing a longish waxed tuft on his shaven head, he is always carrying a single-string musical instrument called a tanpura*). **He is a legendary figure in heaven and on earth, a strange blend of a learned man and a jester, a benevolent mischief-maker, notorious for creating conflict between individuals that hopefully results in essential truth.**

Godse: (*In black cotton cap*) **A young fanatic Hindu, the assassin of Gandhi, he is surprisingly in heaven, as Gandhi desired, that he would be forgiven by God. The assassin believed that Gandhi was patronizing the Muslim minority of India at the cost of the Hindu majority.**

Gandhi: (*Unlike all other characters in heaven, he is wrapped in his traditional loincloth, grandma's iron-rimmed spectacles, and his hanging pocket watch*). **He is a socio-political thinker who evolved a bloodless political technique and nonviolent philosophy to win**

freedom for India from the British. Bored and restless in heaven, he proposes to visit Jerusalem to create peace in Palestine and Israel.

Dr. Albert Einstein: (*In a toga with ruffled, uncombed hair*) Essentially a man of peace and one of the greatest minds in recent history, he is at heart a pacifist. Though he played a vital role in founding Israel, he deeply believed that a Jewish state with borders and even limited temporal power would damage Judaism and might result in narrow nationalism.

Charlie Chaplin: (*Besides his toga, he wears the Hamburg hat and oversized boots.*) A creative genius who acted as an eternal tramp. Though little known, he was part Jewish humanist. He volunteered to accompany Gandhi to Jerusalem only to work for the poor, homeless Palestinians.

Sir Iqbal: (*Besides his toga, he wears his fez cap*) One of the greatest Urdu poets of India, a Persian scholar, and a great Islamic thinker, he conceived the concept of a separate homeland for Indian Muslims. He developed in his poetic work a theme for a pan-Islamic state. In his universal outlook, he shares with other great minds a dream of coexistence of the Muslim world with other cultures and nations. This is based on the self-esteem and nobility of Islamic faith and its message of universal peace.

Plato: (*Besides his toga, he wears long hair and a short goatee.*) *The great* philosopher of classical times who propounded the theme of, *all according to their ability, to each according to one's needs.* He is having an ongoing dialogue with Karl Marx, struggling to reconcile the idea of the commune with the materialistic dogma of Russian Marxism.

Karl Marx: (*Besides his toga, he is seen in his beard and glasses*) The enunciator of Communism in the nineteenth century resents that his utopian theory of a classless society was degraded into a materialistic social order based on Communist Party hierarchy. He is consoled in the fact that, at least for a few decades, the institution of kibbutz created by the pioneering Socialist Israelis practiced the spirit of utopia.

Sarah: (*Seen in blue jeans*) A Jewish Jerusalem teenager who stayed in touch, through correspondence, with a similar young Muslim Jerusalem resident, Leila, since their maiden meeting at a youth camp in Switzerland. They end up co-authoring a book entitled *We the Daughters of Jerusalem–Here to Stay.* She is also known as Shanti, meaning Peace.

Leila: (*In green garments*) Another resident at the Swiss camp. With Sarah and other females, she developed many feminist political views to govern their homeland. She is also known as *Iman,* meaning *Ethics.*

Esther: (*In black pants and a white shirt*) A middle-aged, widowed Israeli wife of an Israeli soldier. She is proud of her fallen husband but equally empathetic to the plight of Palestinian people.

Fatima: (***In black Arabic clothes***) The widowed mother of a young martyr shot by Israeli soldiers. She is in a constant inner-conflict between being a loving mother and a Palestinian citizen who craves human rights. Like Esther, she too was drawn into the underground activity regarding the future of their homeland.

Margarita: (*In grey dress and steel framed glasses*) A mature ex-nun who encouraged Leila and Sarah to stay in touch through correspondence that ended up becoming a published book. She too was drawn into the feminist activities initiated by the teenagers. She is also known as *Resham*, meaning Silken.

Golda Meir: (*In a red scarf of a kibbutz farm*) The Mother of Israel! Formerly Goldie Mabovich, a Ukrainian émigré to the USA who migrated to Palestine in 1921. She was an ardent socialist who spent many years on a kibbutz. She was the Prime Minister of Israel from 1969 to 1974, playing a valiant role as the Defence Minister and Prime Minister.

Dr. Albert Schweitzer: (*In his toga with a colonial hat*) A trained theologian turned a medical doctor who transformed the philosophy of *Reverence for Life* into actuality of life. He was so deeply impressed by a statue called M*elancholy African Negro* by the sculptor of the Statue of Liberty, that he used the location of the statue to meditate on the cruelty of the white man towards the blacks. Years later, he went to Africa to serve the black people *as a penance for the years of oppression the white man* had inflicted. Looking at the statue he had remarked, "His face with its sad, thoughtful expression spoke to me of the misery of the Dark Continent." He also authored *Quest of Historical Jesus* and *The Psychiatric Study of Jesus*.

Emile Zola: (*In a toga, French toque, and glasses almost reaching his nostrils*) The famous French writer of the nineteenth century who shook the French Government with his famous letter to the French President. In spite of years of cover-up by all authorities and popular indifference, he exposed a case of grave injustice to a Jewish military officer. His solitary voice took up the issue at his personal risk. Like no other politician or fighter for causes, he demanded moral justice and roared with just two words, *I Accuse.*

Pierre Eliot Trudeau: (*In a toga and a Canadian winter hat*) One of the most charismatic prime ministers of modern Canada, he removed most of the imperial remnants of a British colony and transformed Canada into a very progressive, multicultural nation.

Lilith: The vivacious first wife of Adam, claiming to be the first born of God. A much maligned seducer of lonely men and evil incarnate in folklores, she has emerged as the darling of modern feminists.

Contents

Act I Scene 1

What the Hell! Gandhi's Killer in Heaven?

(A scene of heaven. A shaven-head man with an unusually long tuft enters with a one-string musical instrument, reciting Gandhi's favourite psalm, Vaishnav Jan real devotee of God feels the pain of others." At the far end of the stage, Gandhi seems to be a meek-looking, black capped man about something.

NARAD: *(To the audience, under a partially lighted stage)* **Welcome to heaven. My name is Narad, and that one over there is Gandhi - I am sure you recognize him. The other meek-looking nobody is Godse, assassin of Gandhi. Yes, you heard it right! Don't be scandalized of a sinner in heaven!**

(There is a long pause).

The ever-forgiving Gandhi prayed to God that he forgive Godse and bring him to heaven. If not obliged, Gandhi warned God that he might go on fast until death! Imagine his nerve to threaten God. We, all in heaven, froze in fear of God's wrath! Gandhi called it *satyagraha*—a moral insistence, or a little kid cajoling his grandpa.

Imagine God rebuking Gandhi that in heaven nobody is allowed to die! Gandhi demurs, "What kind of heaven is it where a simple desire to die could not be fulfilled?" Imagine, after a

1

while, how the Lord, acting in His mysterious way, conceded to Gandhi's plea.

(*Shaking his head in disbelief*) I have never seen anyone with such persuasive power over God. It's amazing! When heavenly residents protested about Godse's presence, God crisply assured them that Gandhi's presence would help in any crisis.

(*Whispering to the audience*) Before I forget, don't buy that fib that I am a troublemaker!

(*With a lower whisper*) They even call me a shit disturber! Just imagine this language in heaven! My divine role is to create healthy debate between various residents. For no fault of mine, it sometimes turns into a wild exchange. To me it is the distilled truth. Truth is not merely bitter; it is crude!

GODSE: Excuse me ...

NARAD: (*Dismissively turning away*) Godse, go away. Don't you see I am busy?

(*In a chatty, confiding tone to the audience*) You know, recently a newcomer politician suggested that I identify myself as a thought provocateur. (*He savours the thought*). Thought provocateur, huh? I like the ring of it! Maybe he is after my vote! Do you think I talk too much?

If you disagree that I don't talk too much , I would arrange for you to quickly visit the galaxy!

(*The remaining stage brightens up showing Gandhi busy at his spinning wheel when a man in ruffled hair enters*)

GANDHI: Come on in, Einstein. I presume you know Godse. He is like my son. How much has he changed since arriving in heaven. No more a fanatic Hindu. Only a great human!

Einstein: Under your influence, not only Godse, we all seem to be changing to be world citizens – children of God...

Gandhi: Of all persons in heaven, Godse admires Iqbal the most, forgetting that Iqbal inspired Islamic Pakistan that infuriated Hindus like Godse...

Einstein: But he did not let you relish the fruit of freedom of India for which you devoted your life...

Gandhi: Godse gave me the greatest gift. Since my departure from earth more than 100 million Muslims stayed on in India (*Impatiently Looking* at one's watch)

Einstein: Why do you wear that? One of the marvels of heaven is the absence of time and calendar, making our existence so light, so unburdened!

Gandhi: ...and above all, thankfully, nobody calls me Mahatma or Gandhiji! Just Gandhi! So real and casual!

NARAD: *(Mumbling to the audience)* But still one can't utter a dirty joke, except to call me a shit disturber! All finks ...

EINSTEIN: I too welcome that informality, Gandhi. No more of that stuffy Doctor or Professor Einstein! Even our outlook is far more universal in heaven.

(Unnoticed a *man in a fez cap enters and begins to chat with Godse)*

GANDHI: *(Confiding)* Great informality and camaraderie ... but after that initial relief from the mission of life, heaven is boring. Don't you feel it?

EINSTEIN: Some Irish playwright described it as eternal death with nothing to do.

GANDHI: Endless boredom. Recently I explored, with a few colleagues, that unique Buddhist tradition of going back to earth to serve the humanity.

It is called *Bodhisattva.*

EINSTEIN: To India, I presume.

GANDHI: No, to Jerusalem.

EINSTEIN: *(With a sweet shriek)* Jerusalem! What do you have to do with Jerusalem?

GANDHI: To initiate the outlook that the whole humanity is our family...

NARAD: (*Whispering to the audience*) ...only to earn millions of air miles between heaven and earth ... and they called him Mahatma, a great soul.

EINSTEIN: (*Savouring*) To Jerusalem! Very intriguing! Gandhi, why? Can I join you to get out of this lifeless eternity, supposedly in the company of million year-old virgins that I haven't met? Maybe they are in another part of heaven!

GANDHI : You are wondering why? To bring peace between the three great faiths of Islam, Judaism, and Christianity in their endless bloodbath! I dream of looking beyond India!

EINSTEIN: Could I join you?

NARAD: (*Confiding in the audience*) Another air-mile admirer!

GANDHI: Shall we organize a group to visit Jerusalem?

EINSTEIN: (*Excited*) Where do I sign? You know how our outlook changes in heaven (*while pointing at Chaplin*). A little too busy entertaining women! After all, what is the use of being in the entertainment world if you can't indulge...?

(*Enters Chaplin*)

CHAPLIN: (*With a bow*) Enchanté to meet you great souls. Heard you are planning a mission to Jerusalem. Not many Americans in Hollywood were aware that I was part Jewish. Being branded a Communist in the U.S. was enough of a handicap. I won't mind accompanying you on this *aliyah*.

EINSTEIN: Gandhi, *aliyah* means immigration in Hebrew.

GANDHI: Immigration! I would like to call it a pilgrimage - a pilgrimage to bring peace between three great followers! To serve poor homeless, landless Palestinians!

NARAD: Chaplin, if you do go, how about introducing some humour in Jerusalem to wipe away some of the people's gloom there? (*Thinking quickly*) How about a satire of an Israeli undercover agent in love with a plain clothed Arab terrorist? You could throw in a Christian to be a party pooper for a love triangle!

(*To the audience*) **Sometimes, I admit, I know why they call me a mischief-maker or worse!**

CHAPLIN: **... and in the end, they are all killed happily. After all, it is Palestine!**

EINSTEIN: **As a token of his penance, Mozart could compose some tunes for Martin Luther to render—as two anti-Jewish figures jointly to repent ...**

NARAD: **I had a comedy in mind, not a torture. To listen to harsh Luther again!**

GANDHI: (*Intervening*) **Friends, before this cultural fête we need to create an atmosphere of innate nobility of these three Faiths to heal their bruised pride. Let us go for a walk and line up our pilgrimage.**

(*All exit except Narad*)

NARAD: (***To the audience***) **Ready for the visit to the Galaxy I promised? I don't forget—I remember with vengance. Remember, it is a heavenly benefit of wine, dining, and dances with sparkly stars for spiritual elation to flush out all the human pettiness. Interested?** (*Disappointed by the silence*) **In heaven, such stony silence means consent! Let us get ready.**

(*Undeterred by the continued disinterest, Narad proceeds with a deep, long breath*).

(*Shyly*) **Please close your eyes gently; take a deep breath and relax.**

(*After a long pause*) **Fantasize basking on a sunny beach with a kind of self-imposed amnesia. Someone you love and respect is massaging your face - so tender, so warm. Imagine your cat snuggling up with you, or your lover sensually massaging you.**

You feel so safe, so loved. Your eyes feel light, lighter, weightless. He or she touches your head. You feel relaxed, almost blessed. He rubs your neck to remove the accumulated fatigue of your life. Your limbs feel light, lighter, weightless. Keep sipping this unique wine of your *being*.

Before you get any funny ideas, it is your lover. He or she is massaging you, caressing your back to wipe away all the burden of your life, to heal all the wounds. Your back feels light, lighter, weightless. You become pleasantly drowsy.

Now again, he or she is touching your outer legs, leading to your knees, your feet are intoxicatingly wobbly as if you are floating in the air. Like a speck of virgin snow, you feel liberated from the agony of existence, a sublimated soul rising up and up and up. The air has turned into your favorite drug—innocent and pleasantly sinful. You are in the outer space, feeling light, much lighter, so weightless, with an emotional glimpse of *nirvana*.

You have turned into a snow bird! You are far away from earth and occasionally looking back at the globe, seemingly so distant, so remote, turning smaller. After a while, the globe has diminished further into a tiny unpleasant dot in the universe, symbolizing human fragility. On the wings of imagination, you have travelled millions of miles and yet you feel the voyage is so real, realizing that the sun is just another star, even smaller than many other planets. We pass by the Moon, waving at the footprints of Neil Armstrong and his colleague Buzz Aldrin, promising to visit them sometime soon. You have passed by all the eight planets, sensing a warm and bright welcome of the cluster of stars—like a gentle sparkling smile dissolving your slight hesitation.

Oh, this is Galaxy, you joyously cry! You join the stars in their lively dance, savouring your favourite food and drink, mysteriously served. Whatever your human frailty is, it gradually dissolves. Buddha whispers in your soul, "It is Nirvana–Mukti."

Others echo it with the hymn of Salvation-Liberation.

Your soul experiences a blissful vacuum flushing out all bigotry.

Inside this vacuum emerges a majestic rainbow with a dangling rope. You pull it down, turning it into a silky hammock. You keep jumping on it with a kid's abundance.

The soothing music fades away. Like a dream, you are thrilled by your favourite childhood lullaby cooed into your ears while the drowsiness feels like your warm security blanket. You feel sleepy. You have dozed off, in a long effortless siesta!

(*There is a prolonged quiet.*)

Amazing! Nearly eight hours have passed like a quiet brook! You are gently awakened by the soft little fingers of a child on your eyelids. These are the first rays of the rising sun. Not seeing your star friends around, you momentarily feel slightly nervous. However, you hear a reassuring oracle. "You can't see us in the bright sun, but we are always going to be with you. Be aware that you are an integral part of the creation.

Realizing that it was a fantasy and that millions of these sparkling stars surrounding you have vanished with their waving sparkle. You feel a bit cheated. However, you hear a solemn oracle, the soothing assurance of the Creator assuring you: That divine glimpse is for you to reaffirm that you are an integral part of that universal unity to practice the width of wisdom - compassion towards all the living beings, and reverence for life.

After a little musical interlude, you are out of your slumber, back with a new purpose to bring peace on earth.

You start your return journey to earth at a multiple of the speed of light. Eventually, you arrive back. With a gentle thud, you touch the Mother Earth and kiss the soil. With fresh reverence, you join the audience.

(Enter Gandhi, Einstein et al)

EINSTEIN: That was a very exhilarating walk, Gandhi, do you always walk so fast?

GANDHI: I am always conscious of time in this endless future! I wonder why I walk so fast.

NARAD: (*Conferring with the audience*) Though kicked of life mercilessly, it is just as well. Had he survived he would never have realized ...

GODSE: (*Godse interrupts him*) Gandhiji, Iqbal is here to meet with you. I detained him, as I wished to consult with him about the Islamic views on the purpose of life and death.

(Iqbal *enters and comes forward*)

GANDHI: Einstein and Chaplin, Meet Sir Mohamed Iqbal, (*quickly correcting himself,*) I mean Iqbal. Sorry, force of habit. Iqbal is one of the world's greatest poets, a Persian scholar, and a great Islamic thinker.

IQBAL: Good correction, Gandhi. I would have to call you Gandhiji as Godse insists doing. Nice meeting you both. Einstein, like your place in the history of Israel, I am also the so-called absentee founder of Pakistan. Narad briefed me about this mission to Jerusalem. Let us hope we can create an atmosphere of *sulah*—I mean peace.

CHAPLIN: But let it be *peace with bread!* Let us help Palestinians rehabilitate on their reclaimed land as we did with Russian and Polish migrants on the kibbutz.

EINSTEIN: ... first making sure to coin the Arabic term for kibbutz! In such a kibbutz, they may not need aid and arms from various rulers exploiting the Palestinian struggle to divert the attention of their own disillusioned citizens. Religion is not a mere opiate of the masses; it is sweet poison.

GANDHI: Religion is the sublimation of our soul, not an excuse to degrade and condemn. Let the Jewish people initiate peace efforts with their own Arab population to share rather than dominate.

NARAD: (*Whispering to the audience*) To take hot air out of all the neighbouring despots. This is Gandhi, the vintage politician.

(To the audience, with a wink) **Never trust a saint!**

CHAPLIN: In return, the Palestinians could genuinely recognize *Israel's right to exist.*

IQBAL: People on earth won't believe that once in heaven, we can be free from religious vulgarity, yet sound so humane and refined. This is real ethics, *iman* in the Muslim world.

GANDHI: *(To Einstein)* As in a Persian poem, it relates: *If there is heaven on earth, it is here, it is here, it is here.* We could recreate heaven in Jerusalem.

IQBAL: Only if the world stops treating Palestinians as orphans and in return, the Palestinian masses assert their pride.

CHAPLIN: Iqbal, years ago, when I was struggling in my career, somebody quoted your famous couplet. "Raise your dignity to such a sublime height that even God Almighty, while writing your fate, may inquire, 'What would you like to be, my child?'"

GANDHI: Dear Iqbal, may I quote another of your poems? "Religion does not preach to fight with your brothers." It sounds better in Urdu, *"Mazhab Nahi sikhata apas me bair rakhna."*

IQBAL: Thank you both. Chaplin I always felt a pang while watching you in your role as Little Tramp fighting for his dignity. To me, the Palestine issue is a struggle for human dignity, not a religious war. Gandhi, as you once said, *"A nation is judged by the way it treats its minorities."* This is a unique opportunity for the Israelis to practice that noble ideal.

GANDHI: To Palestinians I may prompt, "You need no intermediaries between you and Allah to preside over your own destiny." It sounds so profound! I could drink to that!

NARAD: *(Confiding in the audience)* A closet drinker!

(To Gandhi) What is your preference?

GANDHI: Rumi.

NARAD: You mean Rum?

GANDHI: For a learned man, Narad, you are ignorant of Sufi poet Rumi? A great Persian poet of the thirteenth century who addressed God as his beloved!

NARAD: (*Confiding in the audience*) Let us have Rumi on the rocks!

GANDHI: Narad, allow me to recite a couplet of Rumi.

If someone asks
How did Jesus bring one back to life?
Don't say a word
Just kiss him softly on the cheeks.
Like this.

IQBAL: Let this be the anthem of our dreamland, Federation of Palestine-Israel or F.P.I. Gandhi intends to speak to all of us.

(*Getting up to leave*) My preference would be the United States of Palestine-
Israel.

NARAD: (*To the audience*) Federation of Palestine Israel! F.P.I. Sounds like F.B.I. to me! Americans would love this! They may join it to retain the letters U.S.

(*Einstein and Chaplin get up to go*)

NARAD: (*Mumbling while looking out*) I normally revere old people but this Plato is ancient!

GODSE: (*Announcing*) Gandhiji, Plato and Karl Marx.

(*Marx and Plato enter, apparently occupied in heated debate.*)

PLATO: Gandhi, Marx tells me that you hold dialogues in heaven like Socrates used to do in Athens.

MARX: Agora in heaven!

GANDHI: Thanks. You are welcome to join our dialogue on the Middle East.

PLATO: I was complaining to Marx that his Communist Manifesto twisted my utopia: *from all according to their ability, to each according to his need.*

MARX: It may be a poor consolation that immigrants in kibbutz transformed the concept into a workable reality.

IQBAL: Even so, within a few decades it degenerated into a local Israeli Apartheid since no Arabs were admitted in the kibbutz, even as farm hand on their formerly owned land.

MARX: All humans have the instinctive need to survive and live comfortably. Palestinians may reject terrorists if they are assured of the prospects of an honourable political set up and material comforts that are able to extinguish the class war.

PLATO: ... While ignoring their Arab allies who had advised them to temporarily leave their ancestral homes to return to their villages once Israel was pushed into the sea. However, if Israel has a right to exist and wants peaceful coexistence, it should encourage Palestinians to repeat a successful agricultural story and resettle themselves amicably.

NARAD: We could appeal to the conscience of Arab oil countries to stop financing the terrorists, and Wall Street to stop floating the Israel War Bonds.

MARX: Appeal? (*Laughing with ridicule*) Oilmen and investors with a conscience? A bad, nay, a cruel joke. (*Winds down his laughter*)

GANDHI: Instead, the reconciled Israeli and Palestinian neighbours could introduce student scholarships to other Muslim states like Turkey and Malaysia, and give grants for writers and artists.

IQBAL: It is ironic that the Arabic speaking Sephardic and other non-European Jews who form the majority of Israeli population oppose the return of occupied land to the Palestinians. The added irony is that they also complain about discrimination by the European immigrants. Do you think Israelis would even look at a proposal for United States of Palestine-Israel?

GANDHI: We would need to make structural changes in the direct democracy wherein those elected are constantly answerable to the electorate and subject to recall for incompetence or abuse of one's office. I hope to confer with Schweitzer, Einstein, and Chaplin on this concept.

(*Waving at Iqbal*) **Khuda hafeez.**

(*To Plato and Marx*) **It means let God be with you.**

(*Plato, Marx and Iqbal exit*).

(*Smiling, Narad walks in*).

NARAD: **Gandhi, let me tickle you a little. On my way I heard,** (*In an announcer's pose and voice*) **"This is Radio Israel. The time is twelve noon, but as a discount to all our listeners, I will say it is fifteen minutes to twelve!**

(*Looking at unsmiling Gandhi*) **Had I not known you, I would have thought that you wouldn't laugh at anything relating to Israel.**

GANDHI: **Actually, tourists from all over the world would agree with me that the whole of Middle East practices bargaining. As a matter of fact, if an inexperienced tourist pays the price demanded without haggling, the trader would be very disappointed and accuse the tourist that there was some catch! Palestinians and Israelis should start bargaining.**

(*Schweitzer has entered*)

SCHWEITZER: **Oh, Einstein and Chaplin have not arrived. Our absent-minded professor has forgotten his appointment here, but I wonder why Chaplin is delayed.**

GANDHI: **We would blame them for the delayed resolution of the Palestinian Israel issue.**

NARAD: **Maybe Chaplin is walking the way he used to walk in his movies, in his oversized shoes , twirling his cane!**

(*Chaplin has arrived in his oversized shoes twirling his cane*)

NARAD: **No Einstein. Once an absent-minded professor… Perhaps he got busy counting all the stars in the sky, his eternal interest.**

(Noticing Einstein entering) **Think of the professor, and the professor is here!**

EINSTEIN: Gandhi, sorry I lost track of time wondering if Israel could afford to defy the world opinion.

CHAPLIN: Yes, but the views of many Jewish thinkers are changing and a significant number of Israelis who are against continued Israeli occupation is increasing.

GANDHI: There is no better way to win over any people than healing them as Schweitzer did in Africa.

(Surprised) **Think of the angel and the Angel is there. Welcome Schweitzer.**

SCHWEITZER: If I may jump in, God and faith, peace and human rights are hollow slogans unless we practice the *reverence for life*. As I was telling Godse the other day, Israel has an opportunity to start with their hundreds of medical facilities to earn Palestinian good will.

GANDHI: Let's not forget that there are Christians and other minorities in the area that could contribute to the proposal of the United States of Israel-Palestine.

(In a dreamy tone) **Here is a sample of the national flag of the Federation with a white vertical bar representing the peaceful and democratic world support and three horizontal strips in Green, Red, and Blue to represent the Arabs, Christians, and Jews.**

NARAD: *(Hinting at Gandhi and addressing the audience)* **Whatever he drinks seems to be working.**

SCHWEITZER: *Reverence for life* was almost destroyed by military and religious leaders.

GANDHI: I agree. If we re-establish the *reverence for life*, a new class of peace-loving candidates would emerge without too much emphasis on their religious identification.

NARAD: *(Whispering to the audience)* **War without warmongers! It's a horrible idea. *Life without strife …***

SCHWEITZER: In such a political scenario, Palestinians will follow leaders who wish to practice the peaceful nature of their faith, while Israelis could revive their dream of being the beacon unto all nations.

MARX: (*Whispering in Plato's ear before his exit*) Each generation develops a new political notion of governance. Since classical times, the world has gone from kingship, democracy and dictatorship. Let us make room for the Republic—the real republic!

MARX: I gather that Gandhi thinks that even the present democracy is suffering from political parties governed by an election war chest rather than by people's needs. It requires fundamental changes wherein people are elected on the basis of their competence and integrity.

SCHWEITZER: I gather that a person should be elected only for one term, to serve society, and not make a lifelong career in office.

PLATO: I also gather that people should have the power to recall, even before the term is over, if elected candidates appear to be lacking in competence or integrity.

MARX: Who had ever imagined that instead of industrialized England or Germany, feudal Russia and China would become workers' states? It is unfortunate that the notion of a classless society of Communism is fading ... even the Cuban experiment seems like it is perpetual power without room for innovation.

GANDHI: Narad tells me that capitalistic system is crumbling all over the world, and that even the United States of America is turning into a socialized economy.

NARAD: (*Interrupting*) ... and the mightiest capitalist establishment is begging for government assistance for socialized economy. The red of Communist China is turning Blue! I think I will pay a visit to Mao and Lenin.

(*Addressing the audience*) **Want to come along? This is a soap opera in heaven.**

GANDHI: Let me add that Russian Communism may have disappeared, but capitalism hasn't won. It is not that the communist philosophy failed; it was Stalin's tyrannical police state that crashed. United States need not be so smug about the kind of democracy sustained by election funds and the intrigues of public relations.

SCHWEITZER: Let us briefly visit a page of recent history. (*Apparently organizing his thoughts*) **In spite of years of cover up by all concerned, a grave case of injustice continued to surface. One solitary voice took up the issue at his personal risk. No politician or a fighter for causes of moral justice, this man, the most popular French novelist of his times roared with just *two words*.**

GANDHI: Just two words?

EINSTEIN: Yes, this famous writer thundered in an open letter to the President of France, accusing the War Office of misdirecting the public opinion and covering up their actions.

SCHWEITZER: If I may add, the government tried the officer and shipped him off to Devil's Island to be lodged in a cramped stone hut. They were given the order to shoot at the slightest attempt of escape.

EINSTEIN: I remember the international uproar. However, even after a retrial, the writer was sentenced to ten years prison. He fled France for eighteen months, and only returned when the trial was finally set aside.

IQBAL: Wasn't the accused officer a Jew?

SCHWEITZER: Right you are. And the roaring writer was Emile Zola. (*Looking out*) **I have invited him to meet with Gandhi ...**

GANDHI: This happened in France, the nation of Liberty, Equality, and Fraternity?

SCHWEITZER: Unbelievable, but true. (*Zola enters*) **Come on in, Zola. I have already briefed friends of your celebrated two words: *I Accuse*.**

ZOLA: **Well, I did my humble best. However, what deeply troubles me is that the victims of yesteryear appear to be the forgetful victimizers of aujuord'hui…I mean today. Look at Israel between the youths' rocks and solid guns! Let each of us confront Golda Meir with our own weapon of *I Accuse*.**

GANDHI: **Zola, if I may suggest your approach in the tone of "*I appeal*," rather than, "*I Accuse*," if we wish to convey Schweitzer's *reverence for life*.**

ZOLA: **Though it was years after my arrival here, I was simply amazed witnessing the biggest empire in history dissolving in a bloodless revolution in India while during the same era, my France created one of the bloodiest theatres of war ever in colonial Algeria.**

IQBAL: **Liberated from our petty politics on earth, we, as citizens of the Universe, should approach all human issues in the tone of European civilization and Islamic nobility.**

ZOLA: **But let us first shake Golda a little!**

NARAD: **God, you are great. We'll witness some heavenly fire work!**

(*All exit except Gandhi and Narad*)

Act I Scene 2

Godse with Hitler!

GODSE: (*Addressing the audience*) **Can I speak to you in confidence? Since my move to heaven, I have been meditating to understand the mysteries of life and death.**

(*Narad, appearing from behind addresses the audience*) **Has Godse told you how he ended up in heaven?**

GODSE: **Oh, eavesdropping, as usual, Narad?**

NARAD: **Godse, I have God's blessing to be a well-intentioned gossiper, to create a controversy for the truth to emerge.**

(*To the audience*) **Wouldn't you like my job to instigate and witness fights and get paid for it? Well, between you and me, when God makes an error, we are supposed to regard it as an act of God that we are not supposed to question it.**

GODSE: (*Turning to the audience*) **It is agreed that the Lord acts in His own mysterious ways, but why does He usually appear to be so vengeful? Have all religious leaders invented that unkind image of God to control human psyche? We need to rehabilitate the image of God as the Just and Compassionate, not the one always testing Job and others in the Bible to ensure our forced faith in Him.** (*After a long pause*) **Or maybe, in spite of all great religious thinkers, we hardly know God!**

NARAD: Not that God has a split personality; humans have interpreted Him as such to govern the masses with the fear of hell? On the second thought, impossible! God couldn't be a grandpa only to spoil the kids and then gently comment about their sins. (*Shaking his head feverishly*) There is no fun in God sounding so merciful and forgiving. No fun ... no fun... no fun. Seriously, you may urge Gandhi to plea with God to abolish hell ... (Winking at the audience) **Disturb the sh.. gunk is my role...**

GODSE: After prolonged meditation, I still believe that there should be no hell, only staggered heaven.

NARAD: Absolutely not. Can you imagine? Without hell, most of the dead politicians on their demise would be homeless. Of course, they would blame Godse for the loss of jobs and the closure of hell.

GODSE: If politicians' stepbrothers, mullahs, rabbis, and priests are disabled from blackmailing pious people with a threat of hell, they will see the real face of God and may read His/Her mind.

NARAD: They would not recognize God if they see Him or Her! God is like that Hindu concept of *Ardha Nari*, half woman-half man.

(*Pondering*) Come to think of it, that would knock the wind out of fanatic feminists.

(*Winking at the audience*) But tell me Godse, how are you settling down in heaven?

GODSE: I am totally baffled! I went to consult Sigmund Freud about my remorse. Not a wise choice! Since then I have been completely lost! Just imagine, Freud encouraging me to question God if the Lord had any dilemma and thus remains formless, invisible.

NARAD: Did Gandhi ever explain his forgiveness for you, Godse?

GODSE: He assured me that there was something noble in all of us, *(shaking his head)* even me! He further explained that if he didn't forgive me, it would keep his wound perpetually unhealed. He added that even the act of forgiveness is really enlightened selfishness. I couldn't swallow that forgiveness heals the wound of the victim. When I was reluctant to accept his philosophy of forgiveness Gandhiji confronted me with a sharp question: Godse, my son, did you expect me to die of dysentery or old age? Narad, I was dumbfounded.

NARAD: This is weird, describing an act of forgiveness as enlightened selfishness! Only Gandhi could be the inventor of such absurdity!

GODSE: Placing his blessing hand on my head, he said to me, "Godse, son, go out and bring the best in you." I started meditating to know the meaning of existence in whatever station of life or beyond.

NARAD: *(Mischievously)* But if we forgive all sinners, why not Hitler and the whole gang of mass murderers? *(Looking in the wing)* Oh, I see Einstein on his solitary walk. Let us confide in him about your wild idea of forgiving Hitler.

(Shouting) Einstein, over here. Godse would like to have a word with you.

(Einstein appears)

EINSTEIN: Yes, Godse.

GODSE: I wouldn't have the audacity to disturb you. It was Narad's idea to hail you. But since you are here ...

NARAD: *(Intervening)* Godse has a most ridiculous idea of pleading with God, of course, through Gandhi, to appeal to God to forgive Hitler! Have you ever heard of such an absurd idea? I could not imagine Hitler, with folded hands, meekly accepting God's forgiveness by saying to God, "Namaste, meaning I bow to the spirit in you."

EINSTEIN: Coming from me, or anybody, it may sound unimaginable. Though, on earth, I had declared that *the only good German is a dead German!* Since arriving here my earlier outlook has changed to be more universal.

NARAD: Come on, this forgiveness is almost revolting.

GODSE: Exactly! Gandhiji's amnesty may torture me eternally. I would rather be in hell without this insufferable endless wait. Had I not known Gandhiji, I would have accused him of a sweet revenge of a saint.

NARAD: *Sweet Revenge of a Saint*—sounds like a catchy title of a play. I should speak to Chaplin, of course that is after I have patented the title. Forgive my interference in your transgression, but didn't Gandhi offer any help with your unbearable guilt?

EINSTEIN: (*Pondering*) Come to think of it, while renouncing my German citizenship, I should have denounced the racist snobbery of a section of that society, not of all the German people. Such sweeping generalizations are unscientific.

GODSE: Excuse me, Einstein. I need your wisdom. I recall Gandhiji said that it is really I who did him a favour. Had he lived longer to witness his followers' deviation from their ideals, it would have been unbearable. Do you see my quandary when I am thrown on the lap of a Mahatma, great soul?

EINSTEIN: How did you deal with your dilemma, Godse?

GODSE: I went back to prolonged meditation for a genuine change of heart - religion in the ultimate sense...

EINSTEIN: Godse, that is profound! A genuine change of heart is religion in the ultimate sense.

(*Preparing to leave*) Excuse me but I have to ponder over what you said. It would help me search for the Mind of God! Godse, feel free to visit me anytime.

(*Einstein starts leaving*)

GODSE: Could you please stay little longer, Einstein, your presence is so comfortable to a troubled soul like mine.

EINSTEIN: Godse, I will join you anytime in your search...

NARAD: Godse, such forgiveness is too thick to swallow, but did you have such change of heart?

GODSE: Occasionally I get those horrible nightmares in the valley of darkness but I am gradually achieving that deep peace. Is that why death is called eternal peace? Narad, did you believe that one's penance could be so sublime? Do you really believe that all sinners should come to heaven to feel the utter turmoil in the company of kind people?

EINSTEIN: Godse, What else could you have done?

GODSE: I approached Schweitzer to understand the philosophy of *reverence for life*. He suggested to create the image of God as one of compassion, called *rehm* in Arabic.

EINSTEIN: What does that word *rehm* mean to you, Godse?

GODSE: To me it means that if human beings were really made in the image of God, let them understand that God is not a rock or a grenade to hurl at innocent bystanders. It is compassion. Lord Buddha was the living symbol of compassion.

EINSTEIN: Godse, you have made so many profound observations that I would like to confer with you soon. Today I have to organize a meeting with Golda Meir, soliciting her support for Gandhi's trip to Jerusalem. Now, if you excuse me, I must go. *(Einstein exits).*

NARAD: *(Winking at the audience)* Watch this! So, when is Hitler coming to heaven, Godse?

GODSE: Thanks to Gandhiji my temperament is fairly even but Nard you disgust me. It is impossible to talk of change of heart with you. ...

NARAD: *(Dismissively)* The first test of Hitler's change of heart is for him to apologize to Jesse Owens for not having shaken hands with this black winner of four gold medals in 1936 Olympics.

(*Addressing the audience*) Never mind, all of you are too young to know about the 1936 Olympics.

(*Turning to Godse*) How in hell did you meet Hitler?

(*To the audience*) Do you get it? Am I ever so funny, wickedly funny?

GODSE: Though I have the privilege of being in heaven, at sunset I have to retire at the entry level just on this side of hell. Hitler's bunk in the underworld is just below my bed. In one of our talks through the floor, I had to warn him that even Gandhiji might not carry enough weight with God for his move from hell to heaven.

NARAD: (*Exasperated*) Though this is getting rather heavy, tell me Godse. Does Hitler still wear that silly moustache and live with his mistress Braun, whom he married just before their mutual suicide?

(*To the audience*) That was some honeymoon! Killing a bride on her honeymoon! Romance, thy name is Hitler! (Spitting with contempt) A mental…

GODSE: If we usually treat those who are mentally sick, Hitler should not be condemned unless treating the lunatics is a mere do-gooders' slogan on earth for civilized nations.

NARAD: Let us keep God as pictured by fundamentalists and not bother to revive Him as merciful and compassionate. Could God be more humane, a mix of the profound and the ridiculous? Gandhi would have said, "God could be what we imagine Him to be."

(*Gandhi enters*)

GANDHI: My ears were burning. Were you talking about me?

NARAD: Not really, just conspiring to keep heaven from turning boringly pious. Godse has come up with some real neat ideas to get a few more sinners in heaven.

GANDHI: Don't call them sinners. It is the hundredth penny that makes it a silver dollar. Godse was that penny that turned me into a greater Mahatma when he assassinated me, though my definition of Mahatma as *insignificant* still stands.

GODSE: (*Addressing the audience*) No wonder God is hiding from the human beings! Recently I read a very interesting play wherein the women of classical Athens, while parading through the streets, were reciting a chorus. (*Mumbling to recollect*) It goes like this:

In the womb of my mind
In the womb of my mind
I conceived a child
And called him God
I, the mother of God,
Me, the mother of God?
No, no, no. I am a mere woman,
And at that - an Athenian woman!

NARAD: God, what is the heaven coming to? Women's lib in heaven?

GANDHI: It is actually a men's lib because the man would not be responsible for her chastity and financial dependency. She would choose her own role in life.

NARAD: Imagine women soldiers! Or the world without war widows ... starting with Jerusalem.

GANDHI: Godse! At the risk of public ridicule, I placed my faith in your innate nobility. I gather that you were in touch with Hitler. (*Stopping Narad with a hand gesture*) Narad, never ridicule a crazy idealist. He is the very essence of fresh godliness. Please finish your thought, Godse.

GODSE: To keep everybody happy, let there be at least a swinging door between heaven and hell for all departed souls to be governed by the honour system to decide where he deserves to belong.

GANDHI: (*After a long pause*) That sounds like a good compromise. I think I will sleep better than I have in a long time. Heaven and hell with a swinging door!

NARAD: You already look sleepy with such mumbo jumbo.

GODSE: But before I do sleep, I have to confide that I had a long chat with Guru Charvak, the great atheist. He advised that Hindus have the freedom to question the existence of God without the fear of dire punishment.

NARAD: Don't count on God's forgiveness. He would punish you for such absurd thoughts ...

GODSE: (*Walking away mumbling*) I still feel that Gandhiji in Jerusalem is a weird idea. Just imagine a fanatic Hindu like me realizing that ascended to heaven from Jerusalem! Now, Gandhiji to descend from heaven to earth!

(*Gandhi comes closer to Godse*)

GANDHI: My good wishes are with you; don't lose your faith in the goodness of God! The goodness of humanity keeps God Alive.

(*Exit Gandhi while Narad stands reverently with folded hands*)

NARAD: (*To the audience*) That was elevator music in heaven. It says I submit unto Buddha.

Act II Scene 1

Zola's 'I Accuse', Now 'I Appeal'

(*Zola enters with Schweitzer, followed by huffy looking Golda*)

GOLDA: Zola, how dare you expect the Prime Minister of the only democracy in the whole Middle East to come to see you? Maybe, even in heaven, it is the man's world!

ZOLA: (*With utter courtesy*) It is nice of you to come, Madame Golda. When Gandhi suggests anything it is a commandment, and so I am going to address you in the tone of I "Appeal," and not "I Accuse."

GOLDA: (*Ignoring Schweitzer*) Zola, of all the people Gandhi should have known what happens when you side with Muslims— (*very emphatically*) you pay with your life! As our first President declared, there is no Palestinian problem once the Arab world recognizes Israel's right to exist.

ZOLA: (*With equal emphasis*) Golda, Israel has a right to exist— but peacefully, if I may remind. Let me see how you handle a compliment. While living on a kibbutz, you inspired to turn a "hopeless, dreary, heartbroken land" into one of the most prosperous lands in the Middle East. My profuse congratulations.

GOLDA: (*Boastfully*) With or without your congratulations, we made it happen, didn't we? So soon after the Holocaust and within two days of the birth of Israel, five Arab nations attacked us "to be drowned in the Arab sea! " *(With a look of contempt)* ... but the sea dried up within a week with our Defence Force.

ZOLA: The old Yankee in you is still very much alive, Golda. Like a real lady, why not first thank me for my compliment and say hullo to Dr. Schweitzer? Then you can go back being feisty ...

GOLDA: ... *(Back to Zola after a cursory look at Schweitzer)* After my earthly life on Kibbutz Merhavia, I need another fifty years to sound like a Parisian mademoiselle! Well, since 1903, we toiled in the kibbutz. Now I regret to notice that the recent generations are turning it into some kind of private property with swimming pools and health clubs. Imagine them exporting flowers and oranges to Europe, and even America! All those years of hard work with hardly any help from other nations ... *(almost contemptuously)* Now the Arabs are blaming us for our success!

SCHWEITZER: *(Intervening courteously)* Thanks for ignoring me Madam, but if I dare interrupt these dispossessed born Arab-Israelis were not hired even as farmhands by the Russian and Polish immigrants, even though these loyal Israeli citizens ignored all the invading Arabs advise to temporarily migrate and return once Israel was crushed.

ZOLA: We can't rewrite history; we can only improve upon it. Maybe dispossessed farmers, if allowed to till the land, could have dissuaded their youths from joining the Jihad. May I emphatically appeal to your goodwill and advise the Israeli Government to initiate an Arab-Israeli kibbutz to help heal their pride and share the Israeli success?

GOLDA: *(Curtly)* Let me correct the world. The land was not snatched from the Arabs; it was bought from the absentee Muslim landlords, many of them living in Egypt. And the other thing ... the kibbutz was initiated by Jews who did not even observe Sabbath in the busy agricultural season. They were Jews only in name.

ZOLA: But the Jewish National Fund which bought the land was granted to new refugees, wasn't it?

GOLDA: But do you think Arab politicians would have ever approved Arab farmers or any Jewish gestures of rehabilitation. I think leaders of all Arab nations have a built-in excuse to keep their disgruntled citizens diverted by keeping the Palestine issue alive. Palestinian-Arab farmers were not interested in farming...

ZOLA: (*Interrupting*) Then you don't know the urge of a dispossessed farmer to till his land. They would have ignored or even killed the politicians for the land they love to till.

SCHWEITZER: If I am allowed to join Gandhi's visit to Jerusalem, my humble contribution will be to repeat my experience in Gabon, Africa where starting from a chicken coup, we built seventy-two hospital buildings. (*With a pause*) By the way, did anybody ever tell you that you look lovely when you're rude and sound like a sweet war song?

GOLDA: Cut that out. Sorry, Dr. Schweitzer, I mistook you as one more Jew-bashing critic of Israel. No real Jew would ever criticize Israel in its struggle to survive in hostile Arab sea.

(*Einstein has just arrived and taken a back seat*)

EINSTEIN: Excuse me but there is nothing un-Jewish about criticizing Israel. For example, an eminent scientist called the, "Conscience of Israel," dared to praise those who refused to serve in Occupied Territories and pleaded that evacuation from the Palestinian territories should be followed by rehabilitation of the Arab-Israelis.

GOLDA: Einstein, the Jewish world realizes your contribution to the creation of Israel. You may be known as the greatest in so many ways, but no man is greater than Israel...

Einstein: ... and no Israeli woman should pretend to be the sole saviour of Israel...

Golda: *(Interrupting)* ... sounding like the blind devotee of Arafat! Einstein... watch it before Israel accuses of you being a partner of Arafat who is being accused of transferring massive funds to numbered accounts. *(Derisively)* So what? To Arafat, *peace* was a cheap slogan, a mere tactic.

Schweitzer: But...

Golda: *(Curtly)* I'm not finished. In spite of tons of monetary aid, his people are still suffering in abject poverty while his supporters live in posh villas outside of Ramallah, dropping their children at private schools chauffeured in German cars ... and before I forget, his lonely wife survives in Paris. What a sacrifice for a newly married young wife to live in dreary Paris! She must be lonely...

(Recovering her breath) Do you wish for me to go on? *(Without waiting for response)* ... And before I forget, he used high school girls, pregnant woman, and mentally retarded adolescents as human bombs. Their bereaved families are invited to a holy pilgrimage to Mecca, financed by Saudi and Iraqi funds. ... and this is their best leader? *(Spitting)...*

Einstein: Golda, This isn't a debating society. Do you wish to have peace for your own people?

Golda: *(With a dismissive gesture)* Do you appreciate why only Jewish immigrants are welcome in Israel - in their ancestral home regained after spending two thousand years as the pariah of the world? There is no use speaking to you all. Excuse me. *(She walks away, expecting to be stopped. She decides to stay on in the far corner, with folded arms and back towards the group).*

Einstein: *(To his colleagues)* She didn't let me remind her that the war of 1967 was not strictly in self-defence. Moshe Dayan admitted in his own diary that it was the kibbutz residents who pressed the Government to take the Golan Heights.

SCHWEITZER: I hope that the man popularly described as the "conscience of Israel," was not a solitary voice in the wilderness.

EINSTEIN: On the contrary, I heard a prominent Israeli urging for reforms and industrialization in the Arab society. It would have cost less than the *"arms to kill."*

ZOLA: I hope Gandhi gets a better reception in Jerusalem than what we got from Golda.

SCHWEITZER: I hope so.

(Narad bounds in).

NARAD: You want to hear a new gossip? In his prayer, Gandhi complained to God against Churchill's cigar smoking. Surprisingly, God commanded Churchill that he may huff but not puff. Since then, sulkily Churchill has disappeared from public eyes in heaven. *(While Zola shakes his disapproving head, others look at the sky out of boredom).*

NARAD: *(Disappointed because nobody laughed at his joke)* I know you guys are all dead, but I still expected a teensy, weensy smile. Don't give heaven a bad name.

EINSTEIN: *(Staring at Narad's sulky face)* Speaking of England, I am sure you have heard of Yehudi Menuhin's violin on earth. He condemned anti-Arab racism as much as anti-Semitism. Though reviled by right-wing Jews, he thundered that 'Israel would never be secure until its Arab citizens were granted absolute equality.' He had told the Israeli Parliament that steady suffocation of dependent people was utterly wrong.

GOLDA: *(Coming forward accusingly)* The Prime Minster of Israel refuses to be ignored. *(With accusatory finger-pointing)* No wonder Jews call all of you do-gooders, *outcasts*.

SCHWEITZER: *(Hinting at Golda)* Let me interrupt for a moment. Chaplin mentioned that, while on earth, Menuhan used to conduct concerts in Arab refugee camps!

NARAD: Though it would kill me, let me be serious. Israel could organize similar benefit nights to build bridges between the two communities and conduct various cultural activities, including the popular *debka* dance competitions all over the Territory.

GOLDA: If you must know, although this land was the birthplace of Jewish religion, the first refugees did not move in for religious reasons. They were socialists. The whole group owned the kibbutz land.

EINSTEIN: If I could quote another eminent Israeli, he had formed a fully integrated political force named Arab-Jewish Progressive List for Peace. He could be the standard bearer in Gandhi's visit.

GOLDA: You guys, with all the brilliance in your own fields, don't you get it? That Jewish attitude was their deep resolve. *"Never Again,"* is inscribed on the Jewish soul forever to be our national anthem. It is our modern *Masada*.

(Eqbal enters)

IQBAL: Golda, I'm Iqbal. Sorry I am a bit late.

GOLDA: Oh, a token Muslim, I guess.

IQBAL: Gandhi had suggested a nonviolent tone, but I would slip a bit and ask bluntly. "Why, in recent years, did it appear to be an Israeli version of Apartheid? Why are Arab-Israelis just tolerated?"

GOLDA: As socialists, we believed that the community as a whole should own and distribute the land according to the need of any group. Each member is supposed to do one's best and participate in this classless society. There could be no Apartheid in our land.

IQBAL: *(Sarcastically)* Oh, I'm sorry. It is the classless society for Jews only. How cruelly funny!

GOLDA: But when every newly born Muslim child is ingrained with the thought of wiping Israel off the map, survival by any means becomes a priority for every Jewish soul. Not once, not twice four times Israel had to fight for its very existence—we are not going for mere basic survival; we are a modern nation with a mighty army. We worship our defenders. *(Salutes).*

EINSTEIN: But isn't it downright risky to build up social psyche that Israel would never lose a war? Could Israel, the victor, show the grace of reconciliation? For overall peace, first Israel could make peace with her own Arab citizens, withdraw the army from the occupied territory and as a neighbourly gesture help build the country of all children of God?

(Brushing Einstein aside)

GOLDA: Narad, do you remember you told me a joke about a taxi driver who refused to accept fare from the backseat driver, stating, "No charge, Mom. You virtually did the driving." (With accusatory finger-pointing) That joke should apply to you all *backseat drivers*! Funny! While in heaven, they are directing Israel how to run their affairs. That is cruelly funny, Iqbal! But we are all wasting our breath. It seems that Israel has to survive on its own. *(With a roar)* And we shall survive. Let me promise you. On that note, I leave.

(Golda exits unceremoniously)

ZOLA: Friends, it was a glorious defeat, the woman fought us all single-handed and won the round. No wonder Israelis describe her as *Our Golda*, or *Mother Courage*. We'll have to regroup our forces.

(The stage gets gradually darker)

Act II Scene 2

We the Daughters of Jerusalem – Here to Stay

(*A young, single woman's scantily furnished room with a big wardrobe*)

SARAH: (*Answering the door*) **Oh, please come on in. I'm Sarah, and you have to be Leila. Any difficulty finding the place?**

LEILA: **A little. Pity we both live in same Jerusalem but hardly know this part... but I didn't want to risk asking a stranger for direction, I felt like somebody was following me ... maybe I am being paranoid! Let me try to remember your face.** (*After a long moment*) **Maybe, kind of remember. Somehow, I feel as if it is going to be a long-term relationship ...** (Hugs Sarah)

SARAH: **Well, after all, it was almost three years ago at a Swiss camp with fifty other girls.**

LEILA: **This is a dream come true. I still don't believe that our long exchange of letters has turned into a book.**

SARAH: (*Incredulously*) **Our book! We, the authors! Thanks to our editor who risked the wrath of her mother-superior to make this come true. We should meet sister Margarita, I have renamed her as *Resham*—silk in Farsi ... and your new name is *Iman*, meaning integrity.**

LEILA: **And you always claimed you don't know a word of Arabic. In that case, you are *Shanti*, peace in Hindi.**

(*Thanking each other with a long hug*)

SARAH: Isn't it sad that, for generations, both of our families have lived in Jerusalem, and yet we feel like intimate strangers?

(*Unwrapping a book from a green scarf*) With my *salaam to my intimate stranger…, my intimate other half…*

LEILA: (*Taking out from her shoulder bag a book wrapped in a blue scarf*) And here is mine with my *shalom*.

(*Both open their gifts with a burst of happy surprise, reading aloud simultaneously*) We *the Daughters of Jerusalem—Here to Stay!*

LEILA: (*Teasing*) But I am ahead of you, I am getting it translated into Hebrew.

SARAH: Surprise, surprise, mine is coming out in Arabic.

LEILA: Well, we'll have to learn to read each other's language.

SARAH: Do you remember how, while we were training in Switzerland, we wondered that if school children in Switzerland could learn more than one language, why couldn't the kids in Jerusalem?

LEILA: (*With a giggle*) Because neither of us have our own kids! (*With a sudden, solemn tone in a hushed voice*) … and we are not going to have any until we have accomplished our mission.

SARAH: Esther has gone to pick up Fatima and Margarita.

LEILA: Having left her Order, sister Margarita has to have a new wardrobe.

SARAH: Right. A new wardrobe to hide herself from both authorities—the Palestinian and Israeli.

LEILA: (*With sudden urgency*) Where are Esther and the gang?

(*Grabbing the phone*) Hi, Esther, (*Laughing*) did the terrorists kidnap you or something? (*After listening for a while seriously*) Oh, my God. Esther, I will call my dad to meet us at the police station. Leila, Esther is in some kind of trouble with the police…

LEILA: How would anybody know about our meeting? I didn't even tell my parents where I was heading. After all, somebody *was* following me here ...

SARAH: *(Casually)* Don't panic. With my father's connections, we'll get them out. Let's go, Leila. Before the phone rang, I was going to propose that we do something to celebrate our reunion ... something like cry with joy and then sneak out for a big, fatty ice cream and rush back before Esther gets here with Fatima and Margarita.

(With their arms around each others' shoulders they exit. (The stage gets dark for a long moment to signify lapse of time. Narad, dressed in female clothes, comes out)

NARAD: *(In a hushed voice to the audience)* ...that hour in the dark felt like an eternity. Can you keep a secret, because I don't have such a nasty habit? I plan to tell Leila and Sarah and their three elder friends about Lysisastra, wherein the women of classical Greece, fed up of their warmongering men folk, went on a unique strike of cutting their men off in their bedrooms until they stop being at war all the time. And guess what? The Athenian soldiers did stop! Anyway, my visit on earth is to sound out women to establish peaceful coexistence. I have already met some liberal Jewish leaders and moderate Muslims to confirm that the silent majority of the masses are fed up with this endless strife.

(While searching for his phone to answer it, he addresses the audience)

Godse, do tell Gandhi that everything is proceeding as planned. Though slightly nervous, these women are excited about improving the education system and gearing it toward better job opportunities for Arab-Israeli youth. ... also looking forward to extensive use of computers for secret contacts to educate the masses.

Also, tell him that Doctors Without Borders assured all cooperation to Schweitzer's proposal. They were a little shy about Iqbal's programs for self-esteem and dealing with other communities without feeling intimidated. But there too, they did not reject the idea. God, (*Turning to the audience*) I hate to say, "I'm ever so good!"

(*Back to Godse*) Look Godse, I have to go. I'll call you later. (*He quickly goes back into his hideout*)

(*Two more mature, but youngish looking women enter, one dressed in Arab dress and the other in black jeans and a headscarf*)

IN BLACK JEANS: Fatima, please sit down.

ARAB DRESSED: Thanks Esther. (*Throwing herself on the sofa*) Thank God it is over, I was so nervous with all that third degree by the Secret Service till Sarah's father arrived. Both the kids were so assertive during the questioning. (*With a patronizing smile*) After such a confrontation how could they stop for a treat?

ESTHER: Fatima, all my acquaintances think Sarah is my younger sister...

FATIMA: Esther. Mine think that Leila is my daughter.

ESTHER: I had told both youngsters that our lunch was on me only on one condition—no politics and no religious discussion.

FATIMA: What else is there to talk about in Jerusalem?

ESTHER: (*Confiding*) Kids seem to have some plan, but are very hush-hush.

(*On hearing a knock on the door, Esther goes to answer and returns with the visitor*)

NEW ARRIVAL: I am Margarita. I somehow missed my ride with you, so I came alone. I presume you are Fatima and Esther.

ESTHER: Fatima and I were looking forward to meeting you.

MARGARITA: I am so proud that their book is translated into Hebrew and Arabic.

FATIMA: (*With disbelief*) The kids, now renowned authors!

ESTHER: Without giving them swelled heads, they are the future of Jerusalem. I feel so proud of being part of their growth. I have a new dream. Leila and Sarah should invite some youngsters from all communities for a party for fun. They could dance and exchange their favourite tapes and possibly form their girls' soccer teams of mixed membership.

MARGARITA: They are welcome to meet at my old convent in the Christian quarters.

FATIMA: Do you think they could handle it?

ESTHER: Exactly my concern.

MARGARITA: Remember, both of you underestimated your young ladies. Just a few years ago they were so naive, now writers with a new fire in their belly!

FATIMA: We always underestimate our youngsters, particularly the females.

ESTHER: Fatima, (*in a hushed voice*) I overheard them talking about a strange woman they just met.

FATIMA: Oh, a strange woman?

ESTHER: I think this is getting intriguing ...

MARGARITA: She appeared from nowhere saying that she was visiting from a far off place to entreat the new generation to create an atmosphere of peace.

ESTHER: God, were you dreaming or hallucinating ...

FATIMA: Thank God it *was* not a man. Both kids have started saying that all the males in power should be replaced by women.

MARGARITA : I had a very strange dream, almost ridiculous.

FATIMA: (*Excited*) Let us have it, so long it is funny and slightly naughty ...

MARGARITA: It was as if some mysterious person was whispering that a Christian doctor, a Muslim poet, and a Jewish scientist from heaven were about to visit Jerusalem.

FATIMA: **A good dream with a snag. Didn't you notice that all the characters in your dream are men?** (*With a murmuring grudge*) **… to make a new mess. I'm sure … like my husband, whenever he offered help in the kitchen I ended up cleaning up the mess after him. I used to say that if he loved me, he should leave the kitchen.** (*With a sudden burst of tears*) **And he did … forever.**

ESTHER: (*Hugging gently*) **Fatima, Fatima. You know I sympathize with your loss. All the more, he was shot by a hit and run car. You never knew why? Was it because his wife worked for a Jewish family?**

FATIMA: **As if that was not enough, the police shot my son for throwing a stone at a soldier! Where is God?**

ESTHER: **Two sisters trying to comfort each other. As you know, my husband died on guard duty at a yeshivas.** (*Exchanging another long hug*).

MARGARITA: **The only connection to my dream was an ad on our church bulletin board inviting women volunteers for a non-religious activity. Surprisingly, with no request for funds or the mailbox to reply. The advertiser signed some strange name, 'Narad'.**

ESTHER: **Did you notice that visiting men were from different religions?**

MARGARITA: **I also had an anonymous call on my cellular asking if I would be interested in organizing some women's activities since I had helped write the book: *We the Daughters of Jerusalem–Here to Stay*. Though it does convey the strong will of women and their spirit, I thought it was a crank call and so I hung up.**

NARAD: (*Softly coming out from his hideout to whisper to the audience*) **Ask her why she didn't tell the caller to hold on till she gets herself some coffee and a cigarette and say, "I like an obscene caller, please continue."**

FATIMA: This sounds creepy, because I had overheard the same name in chat between Leila and Sarah.

ESTHER: Sarah asked me if I knew anyone named Narad. He made an unusual suggestion that mothers of Palestinian martyrs and the widows of Israeli soldiers should organize a group called "Women Demand Peace, Now."

MARGARITA: Why don't we stage a play on this fantasy?

ESTHER: (*Suddenly realizing but mumbling to herself*) Where on earth are the girls?

FATIMA: I realize that my teenage son gave his life for our religion. May he rest in peace. But I suffer from frequent nightmares. Why *my son*? I feel guilty that my family gets financial support from authorities for his sacrifice, and that we were paid to take a pilgrimage to Mecca. I wish I were with him instead of getting the money and respect of a martyr's mother. (*Pacing up and down*) I am lost. (*Touching Esther on the shoulder*) It is a great relief to confide in you though my people would kill me for speaking to the *enemy!*

ESTHER: I too feel torn. On the one hand, I am proud that my husband died for our Jewish homeland so that nobody on earth could ever humiliate us or shun us. After centuries, we have our homeland. But in my lonely moments, I wish he were alive. (*After a long pause*) But why couldn't two neighbours live peacefully like in earlier generations?

FATIMA: However, when I see the arrogance of Jewish soldiers humiliating poor Arabs or the cunning Arab politicians encouraging poor people's young sons to die while their own children ride in imported cars to private schools, I am lost.

(*Holding Esther's hand*) Is my anger, my love as a mother, my weakness?

ESTHER: Mother's love is never a weakness. Never, never, never.

FATIMA: But it is an endless saga. Somebody should do something about it.

ESTHER: Like who? Should we the women—Palestinian or Jewish—remain decorated dummies that we are all trained to be? To me, it isn't a religious war; it is greed for land and power for men.

FATIMA: I have another son, badly hurt, existing on painkillers. I am scared to death that they would somehow get him too.

ESTHER: (*With slight sadness*) I realize that in Jewish homes, we get relatively better medical treatment but I can't help noticing that the Palestinian women doing our domestic chores do not have much to show as Israeli citizens.

FATIMA: The tragedy of the whole situation is that only women happen to suffer, not their men. At least not as much as the men do.

ESTHER: (*With a nervous giggle*) Without getting into any trouble with either of the authorities, our chat is slightly creepy but exciting.

(*On the way to answer the door the phone rings for Esther to answer. Fatima whispers to ask if she should let the person in*)

ESTHER: (*Resuming his phone conversation*) Oh, Sarah, I am relieved to hear your voice. (*Giggling*) For a while I thought you were kidnapped…

FATIMA: (*Interrupting Esther*) Excuse me, Esther. There's a strange woman at the door wishing to speak to us. Should I let her in?

(*Esther nods with her head to let her in*).

NARAD: Let me assure you that I am a well-wisher from a far off place and wish to speak to you both about Iman and Shanti.

FATIMA: You must be mistaken. There is nobody by these names.

NARAD: Oh, I meant Leila and Sarah.

ESTHER: What about them? They are on the phone. Are they alright?

NARAD: Some van picked them up from the ice-cream vendor and drove them away while they appeared to be resisting the kidnappers.

MARGARITA: Couldn't be. She was right here on the phone.

Esther: (*Resuming her call*) Hullo, hullo. Disconnected. Something is terribly wrong. But was it a black van with Hebrew lettering on it? (*Demanding*) ...and what were you doing there, and who are you?

NARAD: Wait. Iman and Shanti, as they like to be called, have been doing some solid groundwork organizing youth groups to bring peace between communities. By the way, they call you Resham.

MARGARITA: (*Blushing*) I know... no, no, I don't know what you are talking about. (*Flabbergasted*) Maybe I too have a confession to make. (*To Esther and Fatima*) As soon as I blurted out, "The black van with Hebrew lettering on it," I knew I had goofed. I also know my given name is Resham, and I too have known the whole scheme for a while.

FATIMA: (*Beseeching Narad*) Anyway, where are the girls? Are they safe?

MARGARITA: Yes, they are. The purpose of our meeting today was to share the details of our secret society. We had arranged them to be picked up in the black van with Hebrew lettering on it. But why would they appear unwilling to enter? (*Mumbling*) Something is fishy...

ESTHER: One more confession coming. Sarah had warned me too but I had to pretend as if all this was shocking.

FATIMA: Let me join as the final confessor. Leila had detailed the different youth groups of mix communities they have organized.

ESTHER: But something you said earlier bothers me. If their ride was arranged, and you recognize the black van with Hebrew writing—

FATIMA: Are you dreading what I am thinking?

ESTHER: Oh, my God, the kids have been kidnapped!

NARAD: But who could have known about them? Maybe we are being paranoid.

MARGARITA: No paranoia, this is Jerusalem. You don't trust anybody.

ESTHER: Either they are Secret Service or terrorist group. Neither of them likes any peace efforts.

NARAD: What? In Jerusalem everybody spying on everybody!

FATIMA: If anything has happened to either of them I would kill somebody and then continue to pursue the work these kids have initiated. I hesitated to get involved, but this ... this is no religion ... this is no *iman*.

ESTHER: Isn't it ironic? Only in Jerusalem one is in danger for peace efforts!

MARGARITA: This isn't my Jerusalem. I will go back to my convent.

NARAD: They won't let you back in the Order unless you agree to scrub the floor, accepting to be intimidated till they wear down. Do you want to play in their hands...

MARGARITA: Definitely not. I stick to what I have started.

NARAD: That's my girl. (*Winking at the audience*) She doesn't know what I really mean. Could you guess? I am sure you do because your face tells me that you have a dirty mind.

ESTHER: Wait! We are women. In a crisis we weep a little, but once we have wiped off our tears, we growl for our cubs.

FATIMA: Madam, tell us what we could do.

NARAD: Leave it with me. I know these lovers—a disillusioned Israeli Secret Service agent and an equally disenchanted female terrorist—both very high up in their own organizations. I'll see that no harm is done to our kids. *(Winking at the audience)* See how I have turned to be one of them? Am I ever so good? Leave it to me, ladies. Womanhood is always powerful.

(Esther quietly mumbles her prayer while Margarita crosses her heart.)

FATIMA: Allah O Akbar. *(Margarita crosses her heart while others show their clenched fists).*

Act III Scene 1

Dream of United States of Palestine – Israel

(When the scene opens Gandhi is scene welcoming Narad).

Gandhi: Welcome, Narad. How do I thank you for your efforts in Jerusalem? Do let us know when you are heading for Jerusalem again.

Narad: *(Getting up to leave)* If our Jerusalem mission succeeds, against the protocol of heaven I will call you Mahatma, Gandhi. If you'll excuse me, I need to rest. It was a long trip.

(Confiding in the audience) Look at the mahatma. Air miles could make anyone very gussy, even a mahatma.

(Gandhi waits for Narad to leave)

Gandhi: *(In derisive soliloquy)* Mahatma, Mahatma! Perhaps not too many of them realize how miserably I have failed in preparing India and Pakistan to live in peace. What I could not do with those two brothers, I have to endeavour to do with three badly-bruised cousins: Arabs, Jews and Christians.

Oh God, I need the good will of the whole universe.

(Hearing footsteps, Gandhi moves to welcome Zola and others.)

Gandhi: Welcome, friends.

Zola: We heard Narad is making his way in Jerusalem—with women, if I may add!

IQBAL: Somebody should remind him that he is not French.

GANDHI: It seems promising. He is approaching women of all communities—young Israeli widows, mothers bereaving their lost youths.

IQBAL: Gandhi, on our way here, we agreed that the world has ever been changing and even residents of Jerusalem will have to realize that they can not stop the march of times. Even the mightiest leaderships have toppled against people's will. These leaders have two choices: to keep their people in perpetual misery or listen to the women's voice of reconciliation.

ZOLA: It is all the more interesting that women of all communities are daring to be increasingly involved.

IQBAL: After all, the women are the creators and nurturers. They shall prevail. Israeli politicians will have to be statesmen to realize that the silent majority on both sides are fed up with this ongoing carnage. They won't tolerate being widows and childless mothers bereaving their endless loss. Islamic women are deeply influenced by the cultural notion of consensus while the other communities are guided by the democratic principles.

GANDHI: Blending these sad women would work. Our priority is to educate the masses to effectively express their desire for a peaceful settlement, not be intimidated by terrorists or influenced by a trigger-happy military or power-hungry politicians.

ZOLA: I understand that the Internet could be the greatest liberating force, actually greater than the printing press was a few hundred years ago. Let us plan mass Internet literacy for the women's network.

GANDHI: Peace-loving women of the earth could donate their used computers to educate the women of Jerusalem. Once more, the women of the earth would have to announce that Sisterhood is Powerful.

NARAD: (*Entering stealthily and whispering to the audience*) **Did you notice that this is the *all men's club* conspiring to liberate the women of Jerusalem—not even Golda Meir? Perhaps they think women don't go to heaven. Don't tell these men, they too may opt out of such a dull place! Or maybe these departed women chose not to go to heaven because they had enough of their marital heaven on earth. Maybe they requested God to grant them heaven without husbands. I too love a woman, but not a wife.**

ZOLA: (*Pointing at Narad at a distance*) **I bet he is bragging about women in Jerusalem.**

IQBAL: **If you remember the purpose of our meeting with Gandhi, pray tell because I am a bit confused.**

ZOLA: **We were thinking of the assistance that could be helpful to people in Jerusalem.**

IQBAL: **For a change, instead of American soldiers, the Peace Corps volunteers could visit with a computer and leave the computers behind. The computer mouse is mightier than Zola's pen! Politically, it empowers the women to preside over their own destiny.**

GANDHI: **And above all, it is nonviolent. Do you remember that it was through computers that the short-lived political discussions took place in Tiananmen?**

ZOLA: **Starting with Jerusalem, all areas of Palestine and Israel could acquire that power.**

GANDHI: **The computer literacy and bilingual schools could create a unique job opportunity for the youth as well as the multiracial integration.**

IQBAL: **Einstein is supposed to help integrate public opinion on Gandhi's proposal for the United States of Palestine-Israel.**

ZOLA: **Schweitzer seemed quite excited with the proposal of medical centers in collaboration with Doctors Without Borders.**

This is the surest way to win the heart of any mother whose main concerns are children's and elders' health.

IQBAL: The extensive literacy classes in Jerusalem should be gradually extended to the rest of the Union of Palestine-Israel.

GANDHI: And the beauty of all these projects is that it would cost less than guns. All mothers can be excited to become a strong political force and outwit the terrorists and military forces.

ZOLA: Also, as homemakers, the mothers could teach us how to put our national home in order. Einstein recently remarked that, according to Jewish belief, in every generation, thirty-six noble people serve the community. Let us find them.

(Suddenly appearing, Narad is humming Gandhi's favourite psalm, Vaishnav Jan)

NARAD: *(To Iqbal)* You may recall *Vaishanav Jan.* It says, "The real devotee of God feels the pain of others."

IQBAL: *(Slightly curtly)* That is nice, but I am eager to know if you accomplished the mission to Jerusalem.

NARAD: Quite a bit was accomplished. I hope to visit there very soon. Before leaving for earth, I had a chat with a few female residents about my negotiations with women in Jerusalem.

ZOLA: I presume it included Margaret Thatcher and Raisa Gorbachev.

NARAD: Don't be silly; these are empty wine bottles of yesterday. I spoke to the female leaders of Ireland, Turkey, Philippines, Bangladesh, Sri Lanka, Indonesia, etc. *(With a little shyness)* but nothing as fascinating as … *(blushing)* I have fallen in love with this ex-nun in Jerusalem, though I was in female-role.

IQBAL: Narad, you never stop amazing me.

NARAD: Not only will we have thirty-six doctors in Schweitzer's proposal but also we should borrow seventy-two heavenly nymphs to comfort the patients. *(Whispering to the audience)* That means many more fake admissions. *(Suddenly recalling something)* I'll be back. *(Rushes out hurriedly)*.

IQBAL: I like the shape our efforts are taking. If Khadijah, Prophet Mohammad's wife, could be a successful businesswoman and provide solid support to Prophet's mission, why couldn't all other daughters of Eve follow in her holy footprints?

ZOLA: How little the rest of the world knows about this noble aspect of your faith. The inter-faith meetings of Jerusalem women would educate the world of the nobility of all these faiths.

IQBAL: That reminds me of my recent talk with Ataturk and Nasser who said that the Muslims, particularly Palestinians will have to decide whether to identify with Turkey, Indonesia, and multiracial Malaysia or follow the pattern of Taliban.

ZOLA: Gandhi, we have learned something from you. I am going to go for a brisk walk after a long meeting. Will be back soon.

(Waving at incoming Einstein, Zola and Iqbal exit.)

GANDHI: Welcome, Einstein, how are you today?

EINSTEIN: I have been examining with Iqbal the concept of United States of Palestine-Israel.

(Zola and Iqbal have come back).

ZOLA: We postponed our walk. We were too eager to talk about the United States of Palestine-Israel.

IQBAL: ... and betting if such a Union would end up being a built in a civil war! I convinced Zola that Islam is a peaceful culture. Given a chance, it may be beneficial for the whole world.

EINSTEIN: I too have my reservations about the proposal. Actually, has anyone wondered why Gandhi has not tried building his utopia between India and Pakistan?

GANDHI: Anything is possible if masses get actively involved. With Arafat out of the picture, this is a golden opportunity to establish a new people-based political system in Jerusalem and expand it over to Palestine.

IQBAL: ... and it should include people's power to recall any elected politician who appears incompetent, abusive, or dishonest.

EINSTEIN: What intrigues me about Gandhi's proposal is the element that one could only vote for the community other than one's own. Each candidate will have to be so responsible that he would need the confidence of voters outside of his own community to get elected.

GANDHI: And before one has started compromising his or her one's term of office is over.

EINSTEIN: If the combined votes of all Muslims form a majority in this new Union, the extremists could try again to push all Jews in the sea. But if we follow the Gandhian electoral formula wherein you can only vote for candidates belonging to the other community, the brute majority will not be in a position to ignore the minority.

ZOLA: There is no better way to educate the voters to elect quality candidates without any party label or mindless religious loyalty.

IQBAL: In one's self-interest, the voter would vote for the most efficient and honest person and not blindly for one's own community.

EINSTEIN: Borrowing inspiration from the Grameen Bank of Bangladesh wherein four supporters for any loan borrower are responsible for the repayment by 4 other borrowers. This will bring on the spot auditor of one's political behaviour. We could apply the same principle for political office bearers.

ZOLA: This would create a new political system instead of the corrupt capitalistic system and its political masters.

GANDHI: Encouraged by the recognition they received the Bangladeshi women started thinking of education and occupational training so that their daughters can reduce their dependency on the tyranny of males. In Jerusalem, women could be the new king-makers ...

NARAD: (*Suddenly coming out of the hideout, Narad quips*) Without meaning to interrupt, it would be called new queen-makers. (*Turning to the audience*) Am I not the best interrupter in the universe?

IQBAL: Come to think of it, materially secure and educated people may prefer peace. Can you imagine Japanese youths becoming terrorists? I don't.

EINSTEIN: On the other front, Narad tells me that Chaplin is quietly busy planning a film on the real life love story between an Israeli Secret Service and a Muslim woman terrorist turned peacenik. I gather he has already been in contact with these lovers.

ZOLA: I understand that he has also done some research with young and old women in peace groups to openly defy the religious and military establishment.

(*A playful looking man enters.*)

GANDHI: Oh Trudeau, come on in.

(*Addressing the others*) My Friends, Trudeau is a relatively recent arrival from Canada.

TRUDEAU: Hullo, everybody! Sorry I couldn't help overhearing the conversation while waiting outside for this new arrival Madhu from Canada. (*Looking over*) As a new arrival, he must have lost his way.

IQBAL: Was Madhu of the Inter-Faith Council who pleaded that governments should represent the cultural flavour of its varied citizenship?

(*Trudeau nodded*)

NARAD: (*Pointing at Trudeau and addressing the audience*) Did you notice that I'm not the only one eavesdropping?

GANDHI: (*Pondering*) **Inter-Faith Council, an interesting theme! Jerusalem could adopt the model and gradually extend it to the rest of Palestine-Israel.**

EINSTEIN: **If Switzerland could consist of four flavours—French, Italian, German, and the fourth one, ...** (*trying to remember without success*)

NARAD: (*Whispering to the audience and pointing at Einstein*) **The fourth one is called Rumantsch. Our genius could perhaps name all the planets in the universe but Switzerland is too provincial for him.**

TRUDEAU: (*Sarcastically*) **The fourth ones were numbered bank account holders.** (*With a roguish smile, shaking his head*) **Just kidding.**

NARAD: (*To the audience*) **He wasn't kidding. For a politician, honesty is a slip of tongue.**

GANDHI: **Without meaning to embarrass our new friend Trudeau, let me peep into the past. Nearly one hundred years ago, the Canadian authorities refused entry to some hundred Indian revolutionaries on a Japanese ship and let them perish on board the ship.**

IQBAL: **But to be fair, Canada has become one of the friendliest multiethnic countries. Trudeau tells me that in Toronto they jointly celebrate Id and Diwali, an equally festive occasion for Hindu and Muslim communities.**

ZOLA: **If archenemies Britain and France could become the founding fathers of Canada, why couldn't—**

TRUDEAU: **Jews and Arabs!**

GANDHI: **Narad informs me he just received a call from Jerusalem informing him that Jewish, Muslim, and Christian women in Jerusalem are organizing secret societies to promote peace.**

NARAD: **Trudeau, I also heard that Arafat was on his way to heaven. Someone whispered that he ran a very personal rule, transferring billions of dollars in his Swiss accounts.**

(*As if it were an afterthought, dismissively*) **Maybe it is just a mean yarn fabricated by his political enemies.**

GANDHI: (*Looking bothered*) **If you all excuse me, I need to go for a quick walk.**

IQBAL: (*To Gandhi*) *Khuda hafeez.*

(*To Zola*) **It means, "May God protect you."**

ZOLA: Where were you with such good wishes in my long fight with the French Government for a victim of injustice?

IQBAL: I was around sprucing up on my poetry in Urdu, enriching it with Farsi ...

TRUDEAU: (*Waiting for Gandhi's exit*) **How come, except for you, everybody here is so dull; nobody talks of wining and dining, women, skiing, or hockey.**

NARAD: (*With subdued tone*) **I'm going to like you, Trudeau!**

TRUDEAU: Likewise. Meet anybody interesting on your Jerusalem visit?

NARAD: Five ladies! With my luck, me in my female role.

TRUDEAU: Can we reach these ladies on your cellular?

NARAD: Are all Canadians so colourful?

TRUDEAU: No. I just chose not to grow up.

NARAD: (*To the audience*) **What a guy!** (*With sudden seriousness*) **These Jerusalem girls are politically very serious.**

TRUDEAU: (*Eagerly*) **... must have been hard to behave in your female role!**

NARAD: Not quite. Two were recent bereaving widows, two avowed singles and the fifth one the ex-nun, is a journalist with a recorder - always asking questions, never answering my hint for a date.

TRUDEAU: So, what did you talk about?

NARAD: Well, confidentially, they have built an extensive network of bereaving Palestinian mothers and Israeli war-

widows who believe that men have made a mess and that females should take over.

TRUDEAU: (*With a smirk*) Didn't you offer to be a volunteer?

NARAD: Actually I did. (*To the audience*) Wish I could explain Ardha-nari...

TRUDEAU: Narad, I must run. Hope to talk to you soon.

NARAD: Likewise. Before you go, Trudeau, I gather that you were a kind of philosopher king.

TRUDEAU: (*Pleased by the compliment*) If you don't leave right away I may kiss you. (*Winking at the audience, he exits while Gandhi has re-entered*).

GANDHI: (*With a sigh of relief*) On my brief walk I realized that the pioneers were Jewish only in name. They were primarily interested in founding a commune without private ownership.

IQBAL: Strangely, within fifty years, all the idealism has nearly vanished in kibbutz. We should start kibbutz with Arab name and women as equal members.

TRUDEAU: (*Coming back*) Did somebody mention Arab women?

ZOLA: All these Semitic cousins would hopefully belong to new the United States of Palestine-Israel...

TRUDEAU: But the concept should not remain a piece of wishful thinking. In Canada, not only the natives, French, and English but more than one hundred immigrant groups are genuinely endeavouring to live in peace with each other. When anti-Semitic arsonists burnt down a Jewish library, all of the communities pitched in to rebuild it.

IQBAL: Could you really integrate people of different ethnicities and faiths into one state?

TRUDEAU: (*Emphatically*) Of course. Since Canada established its multicultural program a few decades ago, parents in British Columbia are voluntarily enrolling their children in French immersion courses.

EINSTEIN: (*A little out of breath*) Then, why couldn't Arabs and the Jewish people place their children in similar immersion courses to appreciate each other's culture?

TRUDEAU: (*To Iqbal*) A few decades ago in Canada, we had an occasion to deal with terrorists. I said, "Watch me." Though conscious of public backlash, in good faith we promulgated the War Measures Act, dealt with terror decisively, and withdrew the armed forces once the crisis was over. We started redressing grievances of French-Canadian citizens.

GANDHI: I am glad you followed up to heal the wounds.

TRUDEAU: We could train Israelis and Palestinians to adopt our national health system and assist Palestinian youths to obtain higher education in modern Islamic countries. If Narad lends me his cellular, I could contact Agha Khan Foundation.

ZOLA: So many have shared their secret admiration of this tiny Israel for establishing a workable democracy.

IQBAL: But...

ZOLA: (*With a gesture to let him finish*) and at the same time our hearts bleed for homeless Palestinians as perpetual refugees in neighbouring counties. It is so confusing.

TRUDEAU: The world opinion was that with personalities like Nelson Mandela, Dalai Lama, Jimmy Carter, and millions of others, the rest of the world need not put up with this perpetual Palestine problem. These dignitaries would be eagerly waiting to offer a rousing reception to Gandhi in Jerusalem.

GANDHI: I have an issue with—

IQBAL: (*Interrupting*) Forgive me but I am dying to share with you the anthem for this occasion that says:

We, all Her children, Humanity our faith /

The garden of peace / The world our home.

It sounds better in Urdu:

Auld Hai Hum uski / Insaniyat iman
Aman ke chaman me / Sara Johan hamara.

GANDHI: Maybe I should express my concern later on. As you have heard, Chaplin and Zola have designed the national flag for the proposed United States of Palestine and Israel. It consists of a vertical white strip with three horizontal stripes of green, red and blue to represent all communities.

TRUDEAU: We should unfurl the flag to get used to the new world of multiethnic entities.

GANDHI: Iqbal, you do the honour of unfurling the flag.

IQBAL: *(Firmly)* I won't do it without Einstein and Schweitzer.

GANDHI: I may have a dilemma sometime soon. By the way, when Palestinian people rebelled against the Ottomans in the nineteenth century, they called it *the fight for freedom,* never a holy war.

IQBAL: Because there is nothing like *holy war* in Islamic tradition. Neither is suicide approved. Jihad is really the struggle for self-purification through agitation for justice, tolerance, and peaceful reconciliation. The Koran is studded with such gems.

GANDHI: What is stopping the reconciliation?

IQBAL: The Palestinians have felt so maltreated that they would rather welcome even ruthless dictators or religious fanatics encouraging suicide attacks.

GANDHI: I also believe that unless Israeli authorities win the support of their own Arab citizens, such a population would have no burning desire to support a system that is selectively democratic.

ZOLA: It is up to the Israeli authorities to create an atmosphere of trust wherein the residents feel they are citizens in actuality, not as a political gimmick.

IQBAL: Citizens of Jerusalem could then convince the rest of the country that they belong to the land of their forefathers. They could then settle down with people of different faiths.

GANDHI: I sense the change of heart even amongst Israeli conservative politicians who are risking their political fate by openly striving for de-occupation.

ZOLA: Leaders on both sides need to admit that violence is never going to solve the problem.

GANDHI: *(Suddenly)* Look, I feel tired and need to go for another solitary walk. Be back soon.

(Iqbal and Zola seem puzzled for Gandhi's impulse for a walk).

(Suddenly appearing, Narad whispers to the audience)

NARAD: Something is deeply troubling Gandhi. I will follow him discreetly. *(Confiding)* God assigned me the job to take care of him.

ZOLA: Iqbal, while admiring your spiritual growth, Gandhi once mentioned that, in the earlier phase of your poetic life, you pleaded that, "religion never preaches to hate one's neighbour." In later years, you dreamt of a homeland for Indian Muslims that separated and was further divided to create Bangladesh.

IQBAL: Bangladesh! *(Reminiscing)* That was the saddest day of my existence; it continues to hurt me that the military rulers of my Pakistan could not respect the language rights of Bangladeshis. Secretly, I continued my penance by reciting the great Bengali poet Nasrul Islam's collection...*Agni Beena*, meaning a Burning Lyre.

ZOLA: How poetic! But you know our penance strengthens our ever-evolving growth? Where are you in your growth presently, if I may ask?

IQBAL: Didn't Gandhi talk about my dream of a pan-Islamic state?

ZOLA: As a matter of fact, he added that since then you have evolved further. He described you as *the music of the universal soul*.

IQBAL: Personally he never described it so romantically...

ZOLA: That is Gandhi. He is reluctant to take credit for the compliment he gives.

IQBAL: (*After a long pause*) I am so touched by his compliment. I wish I could compose something for Arab-Israelis to subscribe the to the theme of democratic pluralism as discussed by many Islamic scholars.

ZOLA: Maybe the Israeli military establishment does not desire peace because most of the recent prime ministers are retired generals. Many of the remaining retired ones end up working in collaboration with Palestine politicians in different ventures. They too may prefer the status quo.

IQBAL: To me, this is the unholy alliance between two camps. The Arab administrators in the occupied territories are also content with their villas with Israeli licence plates to travel unchecked within Israel, and the power to distribute quotas and permits to their own supporters. Millions of dollars from international sources could be jeopardized if the genuine peace is achieved. Why bother?

ZOLA: Or it is bad mouthing by the anti-Arab lobby? Even the successors of the idealist pioneers of the kibbutz have developed their own vested interest in the fertile land these days. They are disinclined to return it to the old Arab occupants and thus continue to vote for the status quo.

ZOLA: Arabic-speaking Jews who settled for generations in countries governed by Muslim rulers migrated to Israel consoling themselves that at least the new white rulers are Jewish. They are not keen to speak Hebrew. They continue to remain under-educated and thus end up being politically less eager to grant any privileges to Arab Israelis.

IQBAL: I hope Israelis realize that in international relations, there are no permanent friends - only permanent national interests. To solely depend on American support is suicidal.

Instead of the American support deterring them, the hostile forces are provoked to recruit terrorists. In this vicious circle the Jewish fundamentalists feel justified in acting like a colonial power.

ZOLA: As the Chinese say when two bulls fight, the poor grass gets ruined - in this case the average citizens.

IQBAL: *(Emphatically)* On the other hand, if dealt honourably, the innate Islamic tolerance could tempt Arab-Israelis to share the prosperity of the new nation. It is already happening in Turkey. They opened a multi-faith complex in the Mediterranean resort of Antalya.

ZOLA: To me, that is Jihad in the original sense to insist for justice. Didn't Gandhi call his fight with the British *satyagraha* - insistence for truth?

IQBAL: I am almost sure that is what it means. Initially, I was very sceptical about the concept of nonviolence in a political fight with the British but gradually I realized that it would be all the more desirable if it includes Christians and others to correct the impression of this being an Islamic-Jewish war.

ZOLA: It was always a class war turned into a religious war.

IQBAL: We Muslims could heal our wounded pride by recalling the great Islamic civilization when the Jewish and Islamic culture contributed to the renaissance of Europe. We could repeat as equal partners as prescribed in Koran.

ZOLA: I wonder why Gandhi took longer walks today. Let us go find him.

Act III Scene 2

Crisis Before Departure

(Before they could start their walk Iqbal halts Zola)

IQBAL: *(Pleasantly)* **Zola, so Gandhi describes my little poem as '*the music of the universal soul.*' I feel complimented. Let me hum it once more:**

We, *Her* children,
Humanity our faith,
In Thy Garden of peace,
This earth, our motherland.
No, it sounds better in Urdu. *(Starts humming)*
Aould Hai Hum uski / Insaniyat iman
Aman ke chaman me / sarah jahan hamara.

(Accompanied by Gandhi, Narad has just appeared)

NARAD: *(Whispering)* **Gandhi, did you notice that Iqbal is turning feminist, describing God as *Her*?**

GANDHI: **And also his last line, *Sara jahan hamara* means 'the whole earth my home.' This is his expanding outlook.**

(Seeing Gandhi, Zola exclaims).

ZOLA: *(Sounding relieved)* **Oh, Gandhi, there you are! God, for a while we thought ...**

NARAD: ... that *he* had left for Jerusalem on a dry run? (*Confiding in the audience*) He would be awarded millions of air miles, can you imagine?

IQBAL: (*Embracing Gandhi*) The whole week without a message ... you got us worried.

GANDHI: (*Apologetically*) I needed time out. I was dreading the thought that my humble visit may turn into a grand reception by Mandela, Dalai Lama, and other celebrities. The world deserves someone better than me. The humanity has suffered enough at the hands of us, the so-called leaders. To raise their expectations once more ... no, no, no. it would be the ultimate cruelty...

IQBAL: Gandhi, with your proven record in South Africa and India, why shouldn't they dream of a breakthrough in Jerusalem?

GANDHI: I have my deep doubt. The well-trenched leadership on both sides in Jerusalem may even sabotage our publicized arrival there. We, the leaders of yesteryears have proven to be giants with feet of clay.

IQBAL: Sweeping them all with the same broom, aren't we?

ZOLA: Give me an example of past leaders who didn't disappoint the masses.

IQBAL: Mandela for one.

GANDHI: A rare case of personal grace.

(*Apparently concerned, Einstein and Chaplin have just entered*)

EINSTEIN: Gandhi, I gather from Chaplin that there was some hitch in our departure ...

CHAPLIN: When I was talking to Schweitzer and Trudeau about the rumour they said, 'enough of such gossip-mongering. Tell us when do we depart with a bang.'

GANDHI: Not quite. We should be quiet workers, not bragging saviours—gung ho to save the world. For the past week, I have been meditating on the whole proposal. Instead of getting on the soapbox we need to quietly work with the masses who themselves have been badly brainwashed to believe that some of these leaders are their redeemer.

NARAD: It is not my style to interrupt but I too heard someone saying, "Why the people on earth would listen to any fossils from history to open their minds and follow their lead?"

IQBAL: (*Haughtily*) Gandhi could never be a fossil. It is the well-trenched leadership in the clergy, army, and politics who are live fossils—too afraid to upset the status quo, too comfortable in their niche to bring any fundamental change.

NARAD: Before Golda arrives, would you like a gossip? (*Without waiting for their response, he proceeds to deliver*) When Israel was on the verge of collapse during one of those Arab-Israeli wars one of Golda's generals gave her a handful of sleeping pills to quietly swallow if Israel fell. Against the imminent disaster, the situation improved overnight and she forgot about those pills and finished her job. I never imagined I would express my admiration for her devotion to Israel.

(*Looking out*) Think of a shrew and there she is.

(*Coughing a bit*) Hi, Golda. Mother of Israel, So nice to see you—

GOLDA: (*Brushing aside Narad*) So, Gandhi, Israel can't count on even one world leader?

(*Trying to calm herself down*) I heard the prattle that the visit to Jerusalem is cancelled. Why?

(*With slight hesitation*) Since I was raised to respect the elders, let me hear you out.

NARAD: (*To the audience*) When Golda is civil, Gandhi should take shelter.

GOLDA: Gandhi, what is this yarn that you are having second thoughts about visiting Jerusalem?

GANDHI: It's no prattle as you put it ...I am questioning my own wisdom to the proposed visit.

GOLDA: (Derisively) **I never had much faith in anybody except our I.D.F.** *(with added emphasis)* **Israel Defence Force.**

CHAPLIN: **Golda, you remind me of one of my movies. It was** *Great Dictator.* **The Great Leader of Germany was so sure, so sure, that one could laugh at his sickness.**

GOLDA: **Chaplin, you're welcome on my list of fools; Narad was not the only one in that Fellowship of Fools. Israel's Defence doesn't tolerate fools.**

EINSTEIN: **In the name of national defence, one need not ever be proud of creating thousands of widows or orphaned children. Their blood taints the nobility of three eminent faiths of Jerusalem. When the sublime spirit of Gandhi struggles to stop the bloodbath, to describe it as a prattle is the saddest moment in Jerusalem.**

GANDHI: **Golda, may I call you sister Golda? Perhaps I did not express my dilemma clearly. None of us are giving up on the dream of peaceful Jerusalem. The visitors from heaven may take vows of silence and prepare the women of all three faiths to bring peace by their own innate goodness to create a new social order.**

NARAD: *(Protesting)* **Why such a low key approach?**

GANDHI: **Because we wish to create the social order wherein no priests or politicians stay in perpetual power to abuse and exploit their citizens. Instead, the State would be run by the nobility of the three faiths practiced in the frame work of democratic values.**

GOLDA: *(Rolling her eyes)* **Dreams, dreams ...**

GANDHI: **Any vision could be a dream. Any dream could lead to a probability, a possibility and ultimately an actuality.**

EINSTEIN: **Like Israel, if a dream of more than two thousand years could be an abode for people of all faiths to share their success in the ever-changing world, why not this dream?**

GOLDA: It is not going to be easy to sell the idea to Israelis ...

IQBAL: It is going to be equally difficult to sell the idea to Muslims and Christians but with the grace of God, insallah, the Muslim word world utter we would wholeheartedly try to accomplish...

ZOLA: The world could look with confidence in the future, reaffirm one's faith in one's cultural background and extend the hand of goodwill achieve peaceful lifestyle.

IQBAL: Though it is a bit scary to reach out to people beyond one's own culture I shudder when I think of today's Iraqi Sunni and Shia quibbling with the Kurds in between. And to talk about a Union of three faiths?

ZOLA: Couldn't the Jerusalem women of different faiths at least try to reconcile to be good mothers, good wives and good humans? Why should religion continue to be the instrument of hate?

These women would invest their energies in humanizing their motherly love for each other's families and relatives.

(*Enter Schweitzer, Trudeau, and others*)

TRUDEAU: We would train women to take over the affairs of the state. If they could run their homes they could surely run the government.

SCHWEITZER: We would open clinics so the women may treat and nurture others.

GANDHI: In the name of truth and justice they would abolish the party system and introduce a new power base...

GOLDA: (*Interrupting*) Look who is talking. Gandhi, a politician all your life now you are out to emasculate the crowd?

GANDHI: Not quite. I wish them to stop being self-appointed presidents for life. Was royalty abolished to create a new breed of abusers?

IQBAL: If nobody could seek re-election, there would be no party slush funds and thus no political corruption.

GOLDA: Can you call them abusers if they are duly elected?

GANDHI: Duly elected! That is a laugh. When too long in power, even the most idealistic degenerate.

GOLDA: Even someone like President Roosevelt?

GANDHI: As against one Roosevelt, how many clinched on to power by any means? Mandela is one of those rarities who voluntarily retired at the climax of his popularity.

GOLDA: Usually those who continue to stay in power do so to respect people's wishes.

NARAD: Like Idi Amin and the present day people *darlings*! Absolute power does not corrupt absolutely; it leaves behind heirs, like those in North Korea and others...

GOLDA: (*Shushing everybody*) Shush. Come to think of it, if one didn't have an eye on re-election, he would not need a large slush fund. I never thought I could ever agree with Gandhi...

NARAD: (*Whispering to the audience*) One of those rare moments when Golda thinks so positively. It is liquid gold, but don't drink it; don't even smell it. It is Golda's gold!

GOLDA: The masses may still not like the dream of the Union of Palestine-Jerusalem.

GANDHI: (*Shaking head*) Masses, masses! Since the days of Russian Communism, the *masses* were only a handy slogan.

GOLDA: You are dreaming but I will let you continue.

NARAD: (*To the audience*) After all, she is well bred. (Snickering).

GOLDA: The people will still vote for their traditional leaders. Apparently you don't know our politics, Gandhi?

GANDHI: Not mere politics, I know human beings who are essentially good; their innate sense of fairness will elect individuals now aware of the voters' power to recall those corrupt, abusive and incompetent.

GOLDA: I am a bit intrigued that you, Gandhi, greater than any democratic thinker in history, is so low key.

NARAD: That is Gandhi who never underestimates the common sense of the people, particularly the women, however subdued they appear.

(*Einstein has just arrived*)

GOLDA: Oh, there you are. I was having a private chat with Gandhi.

NARAD: (*Whispering*) Einstein, don't worry; I am on guard duty.

GANDHI: As I just said to Golda, it is a historic opportunity to change the system wherein the electorate remains in real power.

EINSTEIN: How?

GANDHI: By abolishing the party system with their election funding.

IQBAL: Pardon me.

GANDHI: There should be no nominees, only worthy individuals running for office on the basis of their reputation.

ZOLA: But pray, how do they run their campaign?

GANDHI: The government could fund it. That also disables those in power from perpetuating their hold or nominating their political or family heirs.

ZOLA: How does this apply to your visit?

GANDHI: When we help return power to Palestinians and Israelis, it still won't be power to the people.

IQBAL: Isn't the next election the solution?

GANDHI: What, to give them an added opportunity to manipulate the voters to get re-elected, to stay in power?

IQBAL: What if the elected official proves to be incompetent or dishonest?

GANDHI: People innately know their mass power. Didn't they oust the mighty dictators Marcos of Philippines and Suharto of Indonesia in spite of all the military and police behind them?

As God will advise the voters through Iqbal, *What would you like to be, my child?*

ZOLA: Where to in your vision?

NARAD: To the most cynical concept. Let Gandhi explain.

GANDHI: Let the voters of Jerusalem be listed in four groups: Islamic, Jewish, Christian and of nonreligious political ideologues. They could vote for a candidate from outside of one's own group thus eliminating the blind loyalty to one's tribe, language or religion.

IQBAL: Aren't we going back into communal voting system?

ZOLA: If I get it right, you are likely to vote someone really worthy of your vote by transcending your narrow religious loyalty.

GANDHI: … also by consensus they could select rotating prime minister for one term to prevent anybody monopolizing power.

NARAD: *(With pretended earnestness)* That is not fair as there will be no politicians in hell or earth to ridicule. The greater tragedy will be the lack of numbered bank accounts in Swiss Banks!

ZOLA: But why believe that traditional political leaders would necessarily be without ideals?

GANDHI: They all start idealistically. Take Stalin, he was perhaps a genuine communist but ended up with a police state.

NARAD: *(Suddenly)* Why are you sparing Hitler? Is it because he claimed to be an Aryan like Hindus did for centuries? Or is it that Godse is trying to get him admitted to heaven?

GANDHI: No. For Hitler it would require a special appeal to God to forgive Hitler who turned one of the most sophisticated people in Europe into becoming mass liquidators …

NARAD: *(With feigned protest)* The Nazis did remain sophisticated connoisseurs of valuable art that they stole from

Jews. These Nazis took out all the gold teeth from the people sent to gas chambers. Nazis were only protecting the citizens' property from being buried or sent with their ashes in the gas chambers.

GANDHI: Do I need to remind you that sarcasm is the worst kind of humour?

NARAD: Gandhi, while truth hurts, sarcasm is only a bloodless bite.

IQBAL: Forgive my impatience but are we trying to rewrite history?

GANDHI: No, as I said earlier, we are evolving the next stage of people's meaningful power.

ZOLA: Can we ever educate the voting masses to think objectively, independent of their faith?

GANDHI: If residents of Jerusalem are content with freedom of movement, merit-based jobs, good education, and universal health system, they would be content to prefer security of life to elect deserving rulers.

GOLDA: ... and what is the fib of Jerusalem as the future capital of the Union of Palestine-Israel with Ramallah as the capital of Palestine and Tel Aviv as that of Israel. It won't work ...

NARAD: Not with your charm, for sure. *(To the audience)* I feel someone on earth frantically wants to talk to me. I must call ... *(Leaves hurriedly).*

IQBAL: People may be too cynical to agree to anything like this.

GANDHI: Only initially. If you continue to act with faith, the essential nobility of the masses will prevail.

IQBAL: People are too bitter to be impressed with such tokens, particularly the landless people.

EINSTEIN: We could request that Gandhi's follower who walked thousands of miles to appeal to the big landowners and received thousands of acres for the landless. Trudeau could request help from young Terry Fox who walked across the land for cancer research till he breathed his last.

ZOLA: We could hold a referendum if people wish to live in the United States of Palestine-Israel.

IQBAL: But after all these clarifications, what if we don't agree to your proposal?

ZOLA: What worked in India may not necessarily work in Palestine and Israel.

EINSTEIN: What if all of us demand of you to deal with our followers in firmer tone since not all of them are politically astute to understand the intricacies ...?

GANDHI: (*With a long pause*) Then I don't go.

(*Stunned and whining with muffled anger, they stare at him.*)

IQBAL: Just like that. (*Angrily*) That is utter let down. We won't take it. (*Protesting Iqbal angrily walk out*)

Zola: I'll *accuse* you of bloodless cruelty!

EINSTEIN: How could you build up the whole concept of United States of Palestine-Israel and then smash our hopes. This is dictatorship by a saint!

GANDHI: Respectfully, I am going to follow my conscience.

ZOLA: Then we will proceed to Jerusalem without you, Gandhi.

(*All nod in support standing close to each other*).

NARAD: (*In a loud voice*) People, without being a blind admirer of Gandhi, let me tell you that in one of India's mass struggles for freedom, when two colonial officials were burnt alive, Gandhi put screeching brakes to the whole mass movement of millions that was shaking the very foundation of the British rule. Nearly ninety-three thousand patriots had courted prison and thousands had lost their jobs, homes or land to the Colonial government.

Zola: Didn't the people rebel against Gandhi?

Narad: In their own way they did. The whole nation was angry with Gandhi but he defiantly declared, "I will withdraw from the political scene if you condone these murders. That is not how our struggle for freedom should proceed. You have to so without me."

Though stunned, almost overnight, like a magic wand, the wrath of the nation at this frail-looking man subsided.

Narad: Usually I thrive being wicked and sadistic but not today. (*Earnestly*) May I beg of all of you to abide by him? He needs you as much you need him. Bear with his insistence that our approach should be initially low key. Let the people appreciate that he does not want glory; only ultimate peace.

(*Suddenly wreathing Iqbal appears*)

Iqbal: (*Yelling and pulling out his hair*) This is absurd. Only an ignorant woman could give a bad name to Islam. I wish she dies …

Zola: Iqbal, this is not Iqbal that I know. Is everything okay?

Iqbal: (*Barking*) No. Nothing is okay…

Einstein: Will anybody enlighten us all …

Iqbal: (*Gasping for air*) How could she act like that…

Zola: Who is she and what could she have done to turn you berserk…

Iqbal: Someone informs me that a desperate Palestinian mother was refused help by all Palestinian and Israeli authorities for an operation of her infant except a Jewish father though he had lost his own son fighting armed Palestinians… When the child had recovered, hugging her child she murmured:

'I would raise you to be a martyr – a shahid …'

Can't believe any honest Muslim could be so ungrateful. God, forgive her.

Zola: Maybe God is testing us...

Iqbal: How could a mother her own kid feed such poison... *(Seems to be passing out while others around comfort him.* While all are awaiting Iqbal to recover *some mystical music is emanating from beyond).*

NARAD: *(Going down on his knees, with folded hands in reverence, asking for silence)* This is prelude to a divine message—stand by for an oracle from God.

(After some more music)

GOD'S VOICE: My children, today instead of speaking in Hebrew, Aramaic, or Arabic, let me give my message in your language.

(In a pronounced tone) In whatever corner of the universe Gandhi appears, his majestic modesty will prevail. Really great souls look very ordinary. The strength of Gandhi is in his silence, still silence. Accompany him to Jerusalem peacefully.

My highest blessings for the United States of Palestine-Israel.

I will be with you all, and all the more with my child, Gandhi. Amen.

(Looking above, all reverentially kneel down for God. Before the curtain falls completely, a wild-haired, scantily dressed, attractive woman suddenly bursts out.)

THE WILD WOMAN: *(Looking at the sky)* Not so fast, Dad!

GOD'S VOICE: *(In tired voice)* Now what? Lilith!

LILITH: *(Amazed)* Oh God, I mean Dad, how can you forget about your first Child?

GOD'S VOICE: *(tired)* How could anybody forget you, Lilith?

LILITH: *(Smugly)* How could anybody forget his how the first female on earth **was treated? You know, my woman's instinct was the reason I didn't sleep with Adam on our so-called honeymoon.** *(Demanding)* **How could I give myself to an arrogant man, Dad?**

God, you created Adam and me from the same earth, so why the Hell should I lay beneath him? Such an unfair position could be considered unfair between two equal children of God...

(*With utter pride*) Dad, you have no idea how proud I felt walking out of the Garden of Eden that night! (*Airily*) That was the brightest day and the darkest night of my life on earth and beyond...

(*Walking away only tu turn around*) ...and before I forget, Dad, you favouring the male really changed my image of you...

(*With a roar*) God! You are the one that committed the original sin, not Adam and Eve!

(*Lilith exits while Golda tries to chase her*)

NARAD: (*Addressing the audience*) Did many of you know that Eve was not Adam's first wife?

(*Frustrated by the non-reaction of the audience*) Residents of heaven are no fun! ... and (*with accusatory look of contempt*) ... and you dream and pray all your life to belong to that heaven? This puny prison of perpetual peace?

(*Conferring, Gandhi and others come forward*)

IQBAL: Narad, sometimes you amaze me, calling heaven the "puny prison of perpetual peace." I wish I could compose a couplet that would convey a new glimpse of heaven without its glamour...(*Shaking his head in disbelief*) Adam's first marriage to Lilith would be a universal shocker ....

CHAPLIN: The first thriller ever...

LILITH: Dad, how come you are not saying anything? Dad, Dad? (*Disappointed by his non-response*) Let me try calling you God.

(*Looking around*) Where on earth are you, God? I beg you, don't be the kind of God that is made, on earth, to suit the needs of priests! They would murmur things like, *The Lord moves in His mysterious way* or some shit (*whispering*) ... like that.

NARAD: She whispered *shit* like that.

LILITH: *(To the audience)* Narad never misses a chance to be the shit disturber. He is a *holy* man! My foot! And God, he is your confidant? Nice. Nice choice! I'll pray for you, God.

(Begging) ... Dad, I don't want to lose you again, Ever.

(Very excited Golda enters with Gandhi and others while Lilith walks away as if searching for God)

GOLDA: Lilith, it is unbelievable, but Gandhi and his male colleagues not only welcome a women's mission to Jerusalem, he suggests each one of them present a gift for the women of Jerusalem. Want to know what Iqbal has to offer?

IQBAL: I present my couplet self esteem—*khudi*—that exhorts: "Raise your self esteem to such a sublime height that even God Almighty may ask what you desire, my child." Hopefully it inspires the collective will of women of Jerusalem to preside over their own destiny.

GOLDA: Women of Jerusalem would assert, *We the Daughters of Jerusalem–Here to Stay.* An anthem of awakening for all women!

(Turning to Einstein) Einstein, what do you have to offer for this *aliyah*, I mean the voyage?

EINSTEIN: My tribute! *If there is heaven on earth, it is here, it is here, it is here.* This unique couplet would motivate the women to conceive and deliver such a heaven on earth. In that Jerusalem there would be no need to listen to any

NARAD: These women would murmur: Who the hell would want to go to such heaven where women are not entitled to enter? *(Asking the audience with a smirk)* Hell to heaven. Am I ever so smart!

GOLDA preacher blessing women to go to heaven.: (With a disapproving gesture toward Narad) How about you, Schweitzer?

SCHWEITZER: Since Gandhi has revived the path of *Bodhisattva* to visit the earth I could start numerous health units... I'm sure

God would provide Gandhi a cluster of Oasis on his journey to Jerusalem.

LILITH: (*Suddenly reappearing, whispering*) Narad, don't you dare start a rumour that Lysistrata is hooking up with us to charm Jerusalem women to go out for a night on the town.

(*Turning around*) I got to go, have to pack for my trip. (*Giddily*) I have also to sharpen my wit to destroy the myth of Adam and Eve started by those religious idiots! The real challenge is to break the myth in all religions that sex is a sin and abstinence the greatest virtue! Either God is insane to create the pleasurable instinct or the religions who question the creator! (*Confiding in the audience*) Someday I want to ask Mother Mary to really enlighten me about the virtue of virginity. How could my Dad, the perfect creator, bless us with the joy of intimacy and then punish us for actually wanting to enjoy it? I don't even dare think that maybe, just maybe, God is not as perfect as people on earth really think ... (*Wandering away*)

IQBAL: How do we deal with the Story of Creation? (*Thinking*) Could humanity live without this mountain of melting myth? I am lost.

NARAD: Today we should limit ourselves to the yarn or such smooth noose, so silken that you don't feel it till it strangles you!

SCHWEITZER: Narad, we don't need your morbid drama. People are learning to differentiate between the myths and scientific facts.

(*Huffing, Trudeau enters with Lilith*)

TRUDEAU: Narad called me to come and watch the Greatest Show on Earth. (*Sweetly*) Lilith, aren't you happy that you are not Adam's wife? (*Roguishly*) We, the men, would be too happy to be seduced! Your displacement of men from this trip is femininity at its finest! I'm so happy!

NARAD: *(To the audience)* **Have you ever seen such happy losers?**

GOLDA: *(Interrupting)* **Don't let it sound as if the women are going on a shopping spree in order to grab some flimsy bikinis.** *(With contempt)* **Men! You think it was easy for me to let Lilith head the delegation? I am not cut out to meekly allow anybody else to decide the fate of Israel, with Jerusalem as the capital of the Union of Palestine-Israel.**

TRUDEAU: **Golda, it is the corrupting kindness of Gandhi that you are turning to be so amiable! I imagine God whispering, "I owe you one, Gandhi."**

SCHWEITZER: **Golda, don't you realize that you are being groomed as the Queen Mother—a modern day Mother Mary?**

NARAD: **While in Jerusalem I once opined that Mother Teresa should have been promoted as the next Pope. My Margarita,** *(quickly correcting)* **Sister Margarita had screamed. "Even ten Mother Teresa wouldn't make one Pope. Never, never, never!" The women on earth are women first, not allowed to take over power from men.** *(With added faith)* **This is the mandate of God.**

LILITH: *(With a thunder)* **Then we shall replace God and rename the Union of Palestine-Israel to Women's State of Palestine-Israel. WSPI** *(Savouring WSPI).*

GOLDA: **But we should not get carried away and sounding so arrogant.**

LILITH: **Arrogant? Arrogant?** *(Looking with spite at Golda)* **Look who's talking? Don't be so freaking modest, Golda. For generations, women were brainwashed to be modest because these lions feel castrated by assertive women. How could it be so threatening to real men? When asked, Gandhi's wife asserted that Women in India were given a maxim that "shyness is the ornament of females." 'No more' she proudly added. Our new maxim is** *"my femininity is my ornament."*

LOLITA: Ladies, ladies! I was always accused of sneaking in bedrooms of lonely men. What puzzles me is how these mighty men could always be seduced so easily! (Looking in the sky) ... and Dad, they accused us of being the wicked ones—not these pigs!

GOLDA: We wish the men were lovers, not animals. And Narad, we are training women to bite. Once we have dethroned men, we would invite them as partners.

LILITH: Only if they have refined their soul. God (correcting quickly) I mean Dad, I have always been amazed at how you gave humans the heart to feel, a brain to think, but no actual organ called the mind! I mean, the mind is the seat of our soul to govern ourselves with compassion, Dad.

GOLDA: Amen! Lilith, you are a diamond in the rough. I admire you. Lend us a share of your refined arrogance. Now the women of the world will realize why we chose you as our leader, dear Lilith.

LILITH: I solemnly swear to be more considerate.

NARAD: (Whispering to Lilith) Including your crush on Godse?

LILITH: (Looking at the sky) Could you ever bless me to kill Narad with my gentle dirty look?

GOLDA: This would be the solitary cry of half the humanity made up of females. I have worked all my life on kibbutz with men—politicians, priests, and soldiers. Perhaps you won't realize how difficult my life on earth was, even while I was leading the men. Underneath all their outer admiration I often sensed their concealed resentment for my being a mere woman.

LILITH: Much before her husband was called the Mahatma, he used to be very abusive. Gradually he realized that if a victim refuses to be broken down by violence, the victimizer would feel ineffective almost impotent. In the end, he turned his failure into an effective weapon against the British empire. Mrs. Gandhi informed that as an Indian wife she felt guilty for disclosing details of her married life. All the women on earth have learned to live with males' massive ego trip. Our role in Jerusalem is clear. We shall prevail. Women shall prevail.

GOLDA: We will help Jerusalem women of all faiths to create a new society with or without the help of men.

NARAD: (*Blushing*) I, for one, won't mind working with any of these ladies, particularly with *my* Margarita (*quickly correcting*) Sister Margarita, even if I have to be the Ardha Nari.

GOLDA: (*Abruptly*) Who in heaven is this bloody Ardha-nari?

NARAD: Golda, Golda! You don't know? Ardha-nari is God in the form of half-female. God's energy, his Shakti, his power!

LILITH: (*Confiding in the audience*) When Gandhi lost his power, his wife Kasturba insisted I lead the mission, not her. I hope I am worthy of Kasturba's trust in me.

(*Thinking aloud*) How could His creation like me turn out to be an evil spirit? Neither God is less than perfect a creator nor I that evil. These chicken-hearted scripture writers are giant-faced pygmies. Trudeau once told me that if I don't want to go crazy I should avoid taking these shitty preachers seriously. I just need to know myself and follow my intuition. All women should follow one's inner God.

GOD'S VOICE: Lilith, as usual I was here all the while, quietly watching you all. Let me clarify my role. Many believe that God is neither a male nor a female. Let us imagine a twin-faced doll, depending on which side you happen to look at. That mind is your God within. Follow that intuition.

LILITH: But nobody should pray to and yet blame you. I as your kid cannot stand when priests and politicians exploit people in your name.

GOD'S VOICE: (*With a laughter*) **My kid doesn't have to worry about her Dad.**

LILITH: (*To the audience*) **You are my witness. God called me His kid, second time! As the daughter of God, let me advise you: Don't ever pray. To me, those who pray do so only to ensure their place in heaven. Prayer is the most pious vulgarity of selfish humans. So-called religious people make fanatics, builders of churches, synagogue etc. They are the greatest threats to humanity.**

GODSE: **Forgive my intrusion. If there is God, why didn't He stop me? I can not ever stomach Gandhiji's insufferable forgiveness.** (*Collapses*)

NARAD: **Yes, God, where were you when Godse—?**

GOD'S VOICE: **Narad, you have tortured Godse enough. Leave him alone. His deep remorse is his ultimate panacea. Let me address those who believe in Me. Besides the heart and the brain, there is the mind to bring out the best in a human being. Let that godliness prevail in your head, heart, and mind. Let you be the God unto yourself.**

GODSE: (*Recovering from his lapse*) **Forgive me God but God, my faith remains badly shaken.**

GOD'S VOICE: **If you don't have faith in me, treat me as a psychological prop. Elevate your psych to that sublime height, as my other child Iqbal recites.**

LILITH: (Haughtily) **Dad, this self-righteous verbiage is making me laugh!**

GOD'S VOICE: **At the risk of annoying my dear daughter Lilith, let me smirk at the idea of a women's mission to Jerusalem to reconcile three warring cultures without making peace with these well-meaning men in heaven.**

GOLDA: **As a Jewish person, I am not expected to say the word God, but for God's sake, how do we proceed from here?**

GOD'S VOICE: Accept Gandhi and his colleagues as helpers.

LILITH: Will the male ego let them play the second fiddle?

GOD'S VOICE: Would the female allergy for men allow them to be conciliatory?

LILITH: So, where do we go from here?

NARAD: God could say, "Lilith, go tickle Adam. He is lonely".

GOLDA: *(With folded hands)* You are kidding, right? God.

NARAD: Let me guess. God would say, "Go home and tell a dirty joke to your partner."

LILITH: That sucks, Dad. Narad has no right to mock women. God, do you not take women seriously?

GOD'S VOICE: How could I not take my daughter seriously?

LILITH: *(To the audience)* You are my witness. My dad called me His daughter. *(With added excitement)* My dad called me His daughter. The first thing I will do in Jerusalem will be to read the book *The Mind of God*.

NARAD: Lilith, why don't you share with Godse the belief that the Creator developed in His mind a female child called her Kaam.

(Whispering to the audience) Meaning desire! Godse calls Lilith Desiree when they are alone. Who says Hindu God has no sense of humour?

LILITH: *(With mock anger)* Narad!

(Confiding in audience) For once I don't mind his big mouth. *(Bethinking)* Desiree, Desiree! In recent ages the mistress of Napoleon called her Desiree. The visit to earth is going to be heavenly. God, Dad, you are so kind!

GOD'S VOICE: To celebrate my reunion with my daughter, Lilith, I would love to convey my blessing to the women of Jerusalem. Let Women's United States of Palestine-Israel last for ever. Narad, could you keep this blessing as a secret and not gossip with anyone?

NARAD: *(Solemnly)* **Mum. Not a word, God, I swear!** *(To the audience)* **Be an ideal human, ...go gossip to your heart's desire. This is the chance of your life! With Gandhi in heaven, God is almost turning humane!** *(He kisses the ground reverentially).*

(Iqbal appears conferring with Schweitzer)

IQBAL: (Shaking his head violently) **I wish she were dead - condemned for ever...**

SCHWEITZER: **Who? Why condemn anybody? Why play God? This is not Iqbal I know!**

IQBAL: **Such a woman gives Islam a bad name... that is intolerable... we shall not allow it...**

LILITH: **For God's sake, how could anybody give a bad name to a noble faith...?**

(Intervening Schweitzer who was about to speak).

IQBAL: *(Wreathing with anger)* **I would love to flush out of my mind her memory but if you must know she is a Palestinian mother refused help by three authorities for a critical operation of her child accepted the anonymous help from a bereaving Jewish father ...**

Lilith: *(Puzzled)* **To accept help from a Jewish father to save a Muslim kid? What kind of Muslim you are, Iqbal, to be steaming like this with wrath?**

IQBAL: *(Impatiently)* **No, no. Can you imagine** while **hugging her child for muttering that she would like to raise him to becomes a** *shahid* **– a martyr! It is unthinkable to hurt the saviour of one's child just because he belongs to different religion. It is unforgiveable...**

LILITH: **Doesn't it make you more determined than ever before in our mission to Jerusalem?**

IQBAL: **I am wondering the futility of our mission...**

LILITH: **It seems that the Palestinians are so brutalized that they are allergic to kindness...**

Schweitzer: Have faith in your kindness to melt the hardest cynics.

Godse: I am a moving monument of a ever - suffering soul since brought to heaven. I came very close to Iqbal once I was brought to heaven by none other than my venerable victim.

Chaplin: Not me. I share Iqbal's dilemma to sympathise with a mother grooming her child to be a future martyr?

Chaplin: I am sure that the remaining team of Gandhi mission will have their doubt about going to Jerusalem whether consisting of men or women... Let us postpone the visit...

Schweitzer: Chaplin, what happened to the film maker who reached out to the downtrodden to ridicule Great Dictator with his final solution...

Iqbal: Many of those interested in Jerusalem mission could be reluctant once they hear of my dilemma...

Lilith: (*Fiercely*) What? Are all poets mere finks with finesse? What happened to the poet's role to poetize any noble gesture... or are all men mere wordsmiths? ... but why worry about men? We, the women in heaven are resolved to proceed to meet our sisters of Jerusalem... God? Are you with your daughters? Or are you going to be with men?

God's Voice: I am neither with men or women, I am with the martyrs ...

Lilith: (*Incredulous*) What? I mean God. Let me not lose my faith in you, God! This is unbelievable to hear you utter such words that you are with the martyr... This is a nightmare, I am hallucinating...

God: No, Lilith, it is neither a nightmare or nor a hallucination. Just be a martyr, follow the path of right- jihad as prophet Mohammed defined it to fight for what is just. It is a constant process of inner Jihad means a struggle within – a conflict of conscience. Everyone on earth and heaven should be the part of such a jihad.

Gandhi and Lilith *(correcting)* I mean Lilith and Gandhi, let us go, I am with you.

God: I shall always be with what is fair and right. Amen.